THE FRAGILE
ABSOLUTE

WO ES WAR

A series from Verso edited by Slavoj Žižek

Wo es war, soll ich werden – Where it was, I shall come into being – is Freud's version of the Enlightenment goal of knowledge that is in itself an act of liberation. Is it still possible to pursue this goal today, in the conditions of late capitalism? If 'it' today is the twin rule of pragmatic-relativist New Sophists and New Age obscurantists, what 'shall come into being' in its place? The premiss of the series is that the explosive combination of Lacanian psychoanalysis and Marxist tradition detonates a dynamic freedom that enables us to question the very presuppositions of the circuit of Capital.

In the same series:

Jeremy Bentham, *The Panopticon Writings.* Edited and introduced by Miran Božovič

Alain Grosrichard, *The Sultan's Court: European Fantasies of the East.* Translated by Liz Heron and introduced by Mladen Dolar

Renata Salecl, *(Per)Versions of Love and Hate*

Slavoj Žižek, *The Metastases of Enjoyment: Six Essays on Women and Causality*

Slavoj Žižek, *The Indivisible Remainder. An Essay on Schelling and Related Matters*

Slavoj Žižek, *The Plague of Fantasies*

Slavoj Žižek, *The Ticklish Subject: The Absent Centre of Political Ontology*

Alenka Zupančič, *Ethics of the Real: Kant, Lacan*

Forthcoming:

Alain Badiou, *Ethics: An Essay on the Understanding of Evil*

THE FRAGILE
ABSOLUTE

or,

Why is the Christian legacy
worth fighting for?

◆

SLAVOJ ŽIŽEK

VERSO
London • New York

First published by Verso 2000
© Slavoj Žižek 2000
All rights reserved

The moral rights of the author have been asserted

Verso
UK: 6 Meard Street, London W1V 3HR
US: 180 Varick Street, New York, NY 10014–4606

Verso is the imprint of New Left Books

ISBN 1–85984–770–6

British Library Cataloguing in Publication Data
A catalogue record for this book is available from the British Library

Library of Congress Cataloging-in-Publication Data
A catalog record for this book is available from the Library of Congress

Typeset by M Rules in Cochin 10.5pt
Printed by Biddles Ltd, Guildford and King's Lynn

CONTENTS

For nobody and nothing

One of the most deplorable aspects of the postmodern era and its so-called 'thought' is the return of the religious dimension in all its different guises: from Christian and other fundamentalisms, through the multitude of New Age spiritualisms, up to the emerging religious sensitivity within deconstructionism itself (so-called 'post-secular' thought). How is a Marxist, by definition a 'fighting materialist' (Lenin), to counter this massive onslaught of obscurantism? The obvious answer seems to be not only fero-ciously to attack these tendencies, but mercilessly to denounce the remainders of the religious legacy within Marxism itself.

Against the old liberal slander which draws on the parallel between the Christian and Marxist 'Messianic' notion of history as the process of the final deliverance of the faithful (the notorious 'Communist-parties-are-secularized-religious-sects' theme), should one not emphasize how this holds only for ossified 'dogmatic' Marxism, not for its authentic liberating kernel? Following Alain Badiou's path-breaking book on Saint Paul,[1] our premiss here is exactly the opposite one: instead of adopting such a defensive stance, allowing the enemy to define the terrain of the struggle, what one should do is to reverse the strategy by *fully endorsing what one is accused of*: yes, there *is* a direct lineage from Christianity to Marxism; yes, Christianity and Marxism *should* fight on the same side of the barricade against the onslaught of new spiritualisms – the authentic Christian legacy is much too precious to be left to the fundamentalist freaks.

Even those who acknowledge this direct lineage from Christianity to Marxism, however, usually fetishize the early 'authentic' followers of Christ against the Church's 'institutionalization' epitomized by the name of Saint Paul: yes to Christ's 'original authentic message', no to its transformation into the body of teaching that legitimizes the Church as a social institution. What these followers of the maxim 'yes to Christ, no to Saint Paul' (who, as Nietzsche claimed, in effect invented Christianity) do is strictly parallel to the stance of those 'humanist Marxists' from the mid-twentieth century whose maxim was 'yes to the early authentic Marx, no to his Leninist ossification'. And in both cases, one should insist that such a 'defence of the authentic' is the most perfidious mode of its betrayal: *there is no Christ outside Saint Paul*; in exactly the same way, there is no 'authentic Marx' that can be approached directly, bypassing Lenin.

1   Giving Up the Balkan Ghost

Perhaps the best way of encapsulating the gist of an epoch is to focus not on the explicit features that define its social and ideological edifices but on the disavowed ghosts that haunt it, dwelling in a mysterious region of nonexistent entities which none the less *persist*, continue to exert their efficacy. Coming from Slovenia, part of ex-Yugoslavia, I seem to be predestined to speak about such ghosts today: is not one of the main clichés about the Balkans that they are the part of Europe which is haunted by the notorious 'ghosts of the past', forgetting nothing and learning nothing, still fighting centuries-old battles, while the rest of Europe is engaged in a rapid process of globalization? Here, however, we encounter the first paradox of the Balkans: it seems as if the Balkans themselves had, in the eyes of Europe, the peculiar status of a ghost that haunts it – are not the post-Yugoslav Balkans, this vortex of (self-)destructive ethnic passions, the exact opposite, almost a kind of photographic negative, of the tolerant coexistence of ethnic communities, a kind of multiculturalist dream turned into a nightmare? Does not the very indeterminate and shifting geographic delimitation of the Balkans indicate their spectral status? It seems as if there is no definitive answer to the question 'Where do the Balkans begin?' – the Balkans are always somewhere else, a little bit more towards the southeast. . . .

For the Serbs, they begin *down there*, in Kosovo or in Bosnia, and they defend the Christian civilization against this Europe's Other; for the Croats, they begin in orthodox, despotic and Byzantine Serbia, against which Croatia safeguards Western democratic values; for Slovenes they begin in Croatia, and we are the last bulwark of the peaceful *Mitteleuropa*; for many Italians and Austrians they begin in Slovenia, the Western outpost of the Slavic hordes; for many Germans, Austria itself, because of its historical links, is already tainted with Balkan corruption and inefficiency; for many North Germans, Bavaria, with its Catholic provincial *flair*, is not free of a Balkan contamination; many arrogant Frenchmen associate Germany itself with an Eastern Balkan brutality entirely foreign to French *finesse*; and this brings us to the last link in this chain: to some conservative British ópponents of the European Union, for whom – implicitly, at least – the whole of continental Europe functions today as a new version of the Balkan Turkish Empire, with Brussels as the new Istanbul, a voracious despotic centre which threatens British freedom and sovereignty. . . .[2] Is not this identification of continental Europe itself with the Balkans, its barbarian Other, the secret truth of the entire movement of the displaced delimitation between the two?

This enigmatic multiple displacement of the frontier clearly demonstrates that in the case of the Balkans we are dealing not with real geography but with an imaginary cartography which projects on to the real landscape its own shadowy, often disavowed, ideological antagonisms, just as Freud claimed that the localization of the hysteric's conversion symptoms project on to the physical body the map of another, imaginary anatomy. However, it is not only that the Balkans serve as *Europe's ghost*, the persistent remainder of its own disavowed past; the further – perhaps even more important – point to be made is that precisely in so far as 'the Balkans' function as such a spectral entity, reference to them enables us to discern, in a kind of spectral analysis, the different modes of today's racism. First, there is the old-fashioned unabashed rejection of the (despotic, barbarian, orthodox, Muslim, corrupt, Oriental . . .) Balkan Other on behalf of authentic (Western, civilized, democratic, Christian . . .) values. Then there is 'reflexive' Politically Correct racism: the multiculturalist perception of the Balkans as the terrain of ethnic horrors and intolerance, of primitive irrational warring passions, to be opposed to the post-nation-state liberal-democratic process of solving conflicts through rational negotiation, compromise and mutual respect. Here racism is, as it were, elevated to the second power: it is attributed to the Other, while we occupy the convenient position of a neutral benevolent observer, righteously dismayed at the horrors going on 'down there'. Finally, there is the reverse racism which celebrates the exotic authenticity of the Balkan Other, as in the notion of Serbs who, in contrast to inhibited, anaemic Western Europeans, still exhibit a prodigious lust for life – this last form of racism plays a crucial role in the success of Emir Kusturica's films in the West.

The example of Kusturica also enables us to identify another feature of the Western perception of the Balkans: the logic of *displaced racism*.[3] Since the Balkans are geographically part of Europe, populated by white people, racist clichés which nobody today, in our Politically Correct times, would dare to apply to African or Asian people can be freely attributed to Balkan people: political struggles in the Balkans are compared to ridiculous operetta plots; Ceauşescu was presented as the contemporary reincarnation of Count Dracula. . . . Furthermore, it is as if, within the Balkan area itself, Slovenia is most exposed to this displaced racism, since it is closest to Western Europe: when, in an interview about his film *Underground*, Kusturica dismissed the Slovenes as a nation of Austrian grooms, nobody even reacted to the open racism of this statement – it was OK, since an 'authentic' exotic artist from the less developed part of ex-Yugoslavia was attacking the most developed part of it. . . . *The Balkans constitute a place of exception with regard to which the tolerant multiculturalist is allowed to act out his/her repressed racism.* Therein lies the main ideological lesson of 'the Balkans': when theorists like Anthony Giddens or Ulrich Beck define contemporary society as a 'risk society' characterized by 'global reflexivity', the reference to 'the Balkans' allows us to supplement their analysis by pointing out how, today, *racism itself is becoming reflexive.*

This brings us to another key feature of this reflected racism: it revolves around the distinction between cultural contempt towards the Other and downright racism. Usually, racism is considered the stronger, more radical version of cultural contempt: we are dealing with racism when simple contempt for the other's culture is elevated into the notion that the other ethnic group is – for inherent (biological or cultural) reasons – inferior to our own. Today's 'reflected' racism, however, is paradoxically able to articulate itself in terms of direct *respect* for the other's culture: was not the official argument for apartheid in the old South Africa that black culture should be preserved in its uniqueness, not dissipated in the Western melting-pot? Do not even today's European racists, like Le Pen, emphasize how what they ask for is only the same right to cultural identity as Africans and others demand for themselves? It is too easy to dismiss such arguments with the claim that here, respect for the other is simply 'hypocritical': the mechanism at work is, rather, that of the disavowal characteristic of the fetishistic split: 'I know very well that the Other's culture is worthy of the same respect as my own: nevertheless . . . [I despise them passionately].'

The mechanisms of this reflexive racism are clearly discernible even in today's popular culture – for example, in *The Phantom Menace*, George Lucas's long-awaited prequel to the *Star Wars* trilogy. The usual leftist critical point that the multitude of exotic alien (extra-human) species in *Star Wars* represents, in code, inter-human ethnic differences, reducing them to the level of common racist stereotypes (the evil merchants of the greedy Trade Federation are a clear caricature of ant-like Chinese merchants), somehow misses the point: these references to ethnic clichés are not a cipher to be penetrated through an arduous theoretical analysis; they are directly alluded to, their identification is, as it were, part of the game. Furthermore, the two members of the underwater Naboo people, the comic Jar Jar and the pompously bossy ruler of the Gungans, rather obviously refer to the cari-catural way in which classic Hollywood represented the non-European (non-white) figures of servant and master: Jar Jar is a good-hearted, charmingly ridiculous, cowardly prattling childish servant (like the proverbial Mexican who prattles and makes nervous comments all the time), while the ruler also dis-plays the ridiculously pompous false dignity of the non-European master (again, like the Mexican local warlords in old Hollywood movies, with their exaggerated sense of pride and dignity); what is crucial here is that both figures are not played by real actors, but are pure digital creations – as such, they do not merely refer to clichés; rather, they are directly presented, staged, as *nothing but* animated clichés. For that reason they are, in some way, 'flat', lacking the 'depth' of a true personality: the grimaces of their almost infinitely plastic faces give immediate and direct expres-sion to their innermost attitudes and feelings (anger, fear, lust, pride), making them totally transparent.

The more general point to be made here is the Hegelian lesson that *global reflexivization/mediatization generates its own brutal immediacy*, whose figure was best captured by Étienne Balibar's notion of excessive, non-functional cruelty as a feature of contemporary life:[4] a cruelty whose figures range from 'fundamentalist' racist and/or religious slaughter to the 'senseless' outbursts of violence by adolescents and the homeless in our megalopolises, a violence one is tempted to call *Id-Evil*, a violence grounded in no utilitarian or ideological cause. All the talk about foreigners stealing work from us, or about the threat they represent to our Western values, should not deceive us: on closer examination, it soon becomes clear that this talk provides a rather superficial secondary rationalization. The answer we ultimately obtain from a skinhead is that it makes him feel good to beat up foreigners; that their presence disturbs him. . . . What we encounter here is indeed *Id*-Evil, that is, Evil structured and motivated by the most elementary imbalance in the relationship between the Ego and *jouissance*, by the tension between pleasure and the foreign body of *jouissance* at the very heart of it. Id-Evil thus stages the most elementary 'short circuit' in the subject's relationship to the primordially missing object-cause of his desire: what 'bothers' us in the 'other' (Jew, Japanese, African, Turk) is that he appears to enjoy a privileged relationship to the object – the other either possesses the object-treasure, having snatched it away from us (which is why we don't have it), or poses a threat to our possession of the object.[5]

What one should propose here is the Hegelian 'infinite judgement' that asserts the speculative identity of these 'useless' and 'excessive' outbursts of violent immediacy, which display nothing but a pure and naked ('non-sublimated') hatred of Otherness, with the global reflexivization of society; perhaps the ultimate example of this coincidence is the fate of psychoanalytic interpretation. Today, the formations of the Unconscious (from dreams to hysterical symptoms) have definitely lost their innocence, and are thoroughly reflexivized: the 'free associations' of a typical educated analysand consist for the most part of attempts to provide a psychoanalytic explanation for their disturbances, so that one is quite justified in saying that we have not only Jungian, Kleinian, Lacanian . . . interpretations of symptoms, but symptoms which themselves are Jungian, Kleinian, Lacanian . . . – whose reality involves implicit reference to some psychoanalytic theory. The unfortunate result of this global reflexivization of interpretation (everything becomes interpretation; the Unconscious interprets itself) is that the analyst's interpretation itself loses its performative 'symbolic efficiency', leaving the symptom intact in the immediacy of its idiotic *jouissance*.

What happens in psychoanalytic treatment is strictly homologous to the response of the neo-Nazi skinhead who, when he is really pressed for the reasons for his violence, suddenly starts to talk like social workers, sociologists and social psychologists, quoting diminished social mobility, rising insecurity, the disintegration of paternal authority, lack of maternal love in his early childhood – the unity of practice and its inherent ideological legitimization disintegrates into raw violence and its impotent, inefficient interpretation. This impotence of interpretation is also one of the necessary obverses of the universalized reflexivity hailed by risk-society theorists: it is as if our reflexive power can flourish only in so far as it draws its strength from and relies on some minimal 'pre-reflexive' substantial support which eludes its grasp, so that its universalization comes at the price of inefficiency, that is, the paradoxical re-emergence of the brute Real of 'irrational' violence, impermeable and insensitive to reflexive interpretation.

So the more today's social theory proclaims the end of Nature and/or Tradition and the rise of the 'risk society', the more the implicit reference to 'nature' pervades our daily discourse: even when we do not mention the 'end of history', do we not convey the same message when we claim that we are entering a 'post-ideological' pragmatic era, which is another way of claiming that we are entering a post-political order in which the only legitimate conflicts are ethnic/cultural conflicts? Typically, in today's critical and political discourse, the term 'worker' has disappeared, supplanted and/or obliterated by 'immigrants [immigrant workers: Algerians in France, Turks in Germany, Mexicans in the USA]' – in this way, the *class* problematic of workers' exploitation is transformed into the *multiculturalist* problematic of the 'intolerance of Otherness', and so on, and the excessive investment of multiculturalist liberals in protecting immigrants' ethnic rights clearly draws its energy from the 'repressed' class dimension.

Although Francis Fukuyama's thesis on the 'end of history' quickly fell into disrepute, we still silently assume that the liberal-democratic capitalist global order is somehow the finally found 'natural' social regime; we still implicitly conceive of conflicts in Third World countries as a subspecies of natural catastrophes, as outbursts of quasi-natural violent passions, or as conflicts based on fanatical identification with ethnic roots (and what is 'ethnic' here if not again a codeword for nature?). And, again, the key point is that this all-pervasive renaturalization is strictly correlative to the global reflexivization of our daily lives. For that reason, confronted with ethnic hatred and violence, one should thoroughly reject the standard multiculturalist idea that, against ethnic intolerance, one should learn to respect and live with the Otherness of the Other, to develop a tolerance for different lifestyles, and so on – the way to fight ethnic *hatred* effectively is not through its immediate counterpart, ethnic *tolerance*; on the contrary, what we need is *even more hatred*, but proper *political* hatred: hatred directed at the common political enemy.

2 The Spectre of Capital

So where are we, today, with regard to ghosts? The first paradox that strikes us, of course, is that this very process of global reflex-ivization that mercilessly derides and chases the ghosts of the past generates not only its own immediacy but also *its own ghosts*, its own spectrality. The most famous ghost, which has been roaming around for the last 150 years, was not a ghost of the past, but the spectre of the (revolutionary) future – the spectre, of course, from the first sentence of *The Communist Manifesto*. The automatic reaction to *The Manifesto* of today's enlightened liberal reader is: isn't the text simply *wrong* on so many empirical accounts – with regard to its picture of the social situation, as well as the revolutionary perspective it sustains and propagates? Was there ever a political manifesto that was more clearly falsi-fied by subsequent historical reality? Is not *The Manifesto*, at its best, the exaggerated extrapolation of certain tendencies dis-cernible in the nineteenth century? So let us approach *The Manifesto* from the opposite end: where do we live *today*, in our global 'post . . .' (postmodern, post-industrial) society? The slogan that is imposing itself more and more is 'globalization': the brutal imposition of the unified world market that threatens all local ethnic traditions, including the very form of the nation-state. And in view of this situation, is not the description of the social impact of the bourgeoisie in *The Manifesto* more relevant than ever?

> The bourgeoisie cannot exist without constantly revolution-izing the instruments of production, and thereby the relations of production, and with them the whole relations of society. Conservation of the old modes of production in unaltered form was, on the contrary, the first condition of existence for all earlier industrial classes. Constant revolu-tionizing of production, uninterrupted disturbance of all social conditions, everlasting uncertainty and agitation distinguish the bourgeois epoch from all earlier ones. All fixed, fast-frozen relations, with their train of ancient and venerable prejudices and opinions, are swept away, all new-formed ones become antiquated before they can ossify. All that is solid melts into air, all that is holy is profaned, and man is at last compelled to face with sober senses his real condition in life, and his relations with his kind.
>
> The need of a constantly expanding market for its products chases the bourgeoisie over the whole surface of the globe. It must nestle everywhere, settle everywhere, establish connexions everywhere.
>
> The bourgeoisie has through its exploitation of the world market given a cosmopolitan character to production and consumption in every country. To the great chagrin of Reactionists, it has drawn from under the feet of industry the

national ground on which it stood. All old-established national industries have been destroyed or are daily being destroyed. They are dislodged by new industries, whose introduction becomes a life and death question for all civilized nations, by industries that no longer work up indigenous raw material, but raw material drawn from the remotest zones; industries whose products are consumed, not only at home, but in every quarter of the globe. In place of the old wants, satisfied by the productions of the country, we find new wants, requiring for their satisfaction the products of distant lands and climes. In place of the old local and national seclusion and self-sufficiency, we have intercourse in every direction, universal inter-dependence of nations. And as in material, so also in intellectual production. The intellectual creations of individual nations become common property. National one-sidedness and narrow-mindedness becomes more and more impossible, and from the numerous national and local literatures, there arises a world literature.[6]

Is this not, more than ever, our reality today? Ericsson phones are no longer Swedish, Toyota cars are manufactured 60 per cent in the USA, Hollywood culture pervades the remotest parts of the globe. . . . Furthermore, does not the same go also for all forms of ethnic and sexual identities? Should we not supplement Marx's description in this sense, adding also that *sexual* 'one-sidedness and narrow-mindedness become more and more impossible'; that concerning sexual practices also, 'all that is solid melts into air, all that is holy is profaned', so that capitalism tends to replace standard normative heterosexuality with a proliferation of unstable shifting identities and/or orientations? From time to time Marx himself underestimates this ability of the capitalist universe to incorporate the transgressive urge that seemed to threaten it; in his analysis of the ongoing American Civil War, for example, he claimed that since the English textile industry, the backbone of the industrial system, could not survive without the supply of cheap cotton from the American South rendered possible only by slave labour, England would be forced to intervene directly to prevent the abolition of slavery.

So yes, this global dynamism described by Marx, which causes all things solid to melt into air, is our reality – on condition that we do not forget to supplement this image from *The Manifesto* with its inherent dialectical opposite, the *'spiritualization' of the very material process of production*. While capitalism does suspend the power of the old ghosts of tradition, it generates its own monstrous ghosts. That is to say: on the one hand, capitalism entails the radical secularization of social life – it mercilessly tears apart any aura of authentic nobility, sacredness, honour, and so on:

> It has drowned the most heavenly ecstasies of religious fervour, of chivalrous enthusiasm, of philistine sentimentalism, in the icy water of egotistical calculation. It has resolved personal worth into exchange value, and in place of the numberless indefeasible chartered freedoms, has set up that single, unconscionable freedom – Free Trade. In one word, for exploitation, veiled by religious and political illusions, it has substituted naked, shameless, direct, brutal exploitation.[7]

However, the fundamental lesson of the 'critique of political economy' elaborated by the mature Marx in the years after *The Manifesto* is that *this reduction of all heavenly chimeras to brutal economic reality generates a spectrality of its own.* When Marx describes the mad self-enhancing circulation of Capital, whose solipsistic path of self-fecundation reaches its apogee in today's meta-reflexive speculations on futures, it is far too simplistic to claim that the spectre of this self-engendering monster that pursues its path regardless of any human or environmental concern is an ideological abstraction, and that one should never forget that behind this abstraction there are real people and natural objects on whose productive capacities and resources Capital's circulation is based, and on which it feeds like a gigantic parasite. The problem is that this 'abstraction' does not exist only in our (financial speculator's) misperception of social reality; it is 'real' in the precise sense of determining the very structure of material social processes: the fate of whole strata of populations, and sometimes of whole countries, can be decided by the 'solipsistic' speculative dance of Capital, which pursues its goal of profitability with a blessed indifference to the way its movement will affect social reality. That is the fundamental systemic violence of capitalism, which is much more uncanny than direct pre-capitalist socio-ideological violence: this violence is no longer attributable to concrete individuals and their 'evil' intentions; it is purely 'objective', systemic, anonymous.

Here we encounter the Lacanian difference between reality and the Real: 'reality' is the social reality of the actual people involved in interaction, and in the productive process; while the Real is the inexorable 'abstract' spectral logic of Capital which determines what goes on in social reality. This gap is palpable in the way the modern economic situation of a country is considered to be good and stable by international financial experts, even when the great majority of its people have a lower standard of living than they did before – reality doesn't matter, what matters is the situation of Capital. . . . And, again, is this not truer than ever today? Do not phenomena usually described as those of 'virtual capitalism' (the futures trade and similar abstract financial speculations) indicate the reign of 'real abstraction' at its purest, much more radical than it was in Marx's time? In short, the highest form of ideology lies not in getting caught up in ideological spectrality, forgetting about its foundations in real people and their relations, but precisely in overlooking this Real of spectrality, and pretending to address directly 'real people with their real worries'. Visitors to the London Stock Exchange are given a free leaflet which explains to them that the stock market is not about some mysterious fluctuations, but about real people and their products – *this* is ideology at its purest.

Does this mean, then, that the Marxist 'critique of political economy' provides an adequate account of the process of capitalist globalization? More precisely: how do we stand *today* with regard to the opposition between the standard Marxist analysis of capitalism as a concrete social formation, and those attempts – from Heidegger's to Adorno and Horkheimer's – which view the crazy capitalist dance as self-enhancing productivity as the expression of a more fundamental transcendental-ontological principle ('will to power', 'instrumental reason') discernible also in Communist attempts to overcome capitalism, so that – as Heidegger put it – Americanism and Communism are metaphysically the same? From the standard Marxist standpoint, the search for some transcendental-ontological principle obscures the concrete socioeconomic structure that sustains capitalist productivity; while for the opposite side, the standard Marxist approach does not see how the capitalist excess cannot be accounted for on the ontic level of a particular societal organization.

One is tempted to claim here that, in a way, *both sides are wrong*. Precisely as Marxists, in the interests of our fidelity to Marx's work, we should identify Marx's mistake: he perceived how capitalism unleashed the breathtaking dynamics of self-enhancing productivity – see his fascinated descriptions of how, in capitalism, 'all things solid melt into thin air', of how capitalism is the greatest revolutionizer in the entire history of humanity; on the other hand, he also clearly perceived how this capitalist dynamics is propelled by its own inner obstacle or antagonism – the ultimate limit of capitalism (of self-propelling capitalist productivity) is Capital itself, that is, the incessant development and revolutionizing of capitalism's own material conditions, the mad dance of its unconditional spiral of productivity, is ultimately nothing but a desperate forward flight to escape its own debilitating inherent contradiction. . . .

Marx's fundamental mistake was to conclude, from these insights, that a new, higher social order (Communism) is possible, an order that would not only maintain but even raise to a higher degree, and effectively fully release, the potential of the self-increasing spiral of productivity which in capitalism, on account of its inherent obstacle/contradiction, is thwarted again and again by socially destructive economic crises. In short, what Marx overlooked is that – to put it in the standard Derridan terms – this inherent obstacle/antagonism as the 'condition of impossibility' of the full deployment of productive forces is simultaneously its 'condition of possibility': if we abolish the obstacle, the inherent contradiction of capitalism, we do not get the fully unleashed drive to productivity finally delivered of its impediment, we lose precisely this productivity that seemed to be generated and simultaneously thwarted by capitalism – if we take away the obstacle, the very potential thwarted by this obstacle dissipates . . . (here we could envisage a possible Lacanian critique of Marx, focusing on the ambiguous overlapping between surplus-value and surplus-enjoyment). So, in a way, the critics of Communism were right when they claimed that Marxian Communism is an impossible fantasy – what they did not perceive is that Marxian Communism, this notion of a society of pure unleashed productivity *outside* the frame of Capital, was a fantasy inherent to capitalism itself, the *capitalist* inherent transgression at its purest, a strictly *ideological* fantasy of maintaining the thrust towards productivity generated by capitalism, while getting rid of the 'obstacles' and antagonisms that were – as the sad experience of 'actually existing capitalism' demonstrates – *the only possible framework of the actual material existence of a society of permanent self-enhancing productivity.*

We can also see, now, why the above-mentioned procedure of supplanting Marxist analysis with reference to some transcendental-ontological foundation (the usual way Western Marxists try to respond to the crisis of Marxism) is deficient: what we need today is not the passage from the 'critique of political economy' to the transcendental-ontological 'critique of instrumental reason', but a return to the 'critique of political economy' that would reveal how the standard Communist project was *utopian* precisely in so far as it was not *radical enough* – in so far as, in it, the fundamental capitalist thrust of unleashed productivity survived, deprived of its concrete contradictory conditions of existence. The insufficiency of Heidegger, Adorno and Horkheimer, and so on, lies in their abandonment of the concrete social analysis of capitalism: in their very critique or overcoming of Marx, they in a way *repeat* Marx's mistake – like Marx, they perceive unbridled productivity as something that is ultimately *independent* of the concrete capitalist social formation. Capitalism and Communism are not two different historical realizations, two species, of 'instrumental reason' – instrumental reason *as such* is capitalist, grounded in capitalist relations; and 'actually existing Socialism' failed because it was ultimately a subspecies of capitalism, an ideological attempt to 'have one's cake and eat it', to break out of capitalism while retaining its key ingredient.

Our answer to the standard philosophical criticism of Marx (his description of the dynamics of capitalism should be rejected, since it is meaningful only against the background of the notion of Communism as the self-transparent society in which the production process is directly subordinated to the 'general intellect' of collective planning) is thus that while one accepts the kernel of this argument, one has simply to take a reflexive step back and perceive how Marx's notion of Communist society is itself the inherent capitalist fantasy – a fantasmatic scenario for resolving the capitalist antagonism he so aptly described. In other words, our premiss is that even if we remove the teleological notion of Communism (the society of completely unbridled productivity) as the implicit standard by which Marx, as it were, measures the alienation of existing society, the bulk of his 'critique of political economy', his insight into the self-propelling vicious cycle of capitalist (re)production, survives. The task of today's thought is thus double: on the one hand, how to *repeat* the Marxist 'critique of political economy' without the utopian-ideological notion of Communism as its inherent standard; on the other, how to imagine actually breaking out of the capitalist horizon *without* falling into the trap of returning to the eminently *premodern* notion of a balanced, (self-)restrained society (the 'pre-Cartesian' temptation to which most of today's ecology succumbs).

So where, precisely, did Marx go wrong with regard to surplus-value? One is tempted to search for an answer in the key Lacanian distinction between the *object* of desire and surplus-enjoyment as its *cause*. Henry Krips[8] evokes the lovely example of the chaperone in seduction: the chaperone is an ugly elderly lady who is officially the *obstacle* to the direct goal–object (the woman the suitor is courting); but precisely as such, she is the key intermediary moment that effectively makes the beloved woman desirable – without her, the whole economy of seduction would collapse.[9] Or, take another example from a different level: the lock of curly blonde hair, that fatal detail of Madeleine in Hitchcock's *Vertigo*. When, in the love scene in the barn towards the end of the film, Scottie passionately embraces Judy refashioned into the dead Madeleine, during their famous 360-degree kiss, he stops kissing her and withdraws just long enough to steal a look at her newly blonde hair, as if to reassure himself that the particular feature which transforms her into the object of desire is still there. . . . Crucial here is the opposition between the vortex that threatens to engulf Scottie (the 'vertigo' of the film's title, the deadly Thing) and the blonde curl that imitates the vertigo of the Thing, but in a miniaturized, gentrified form.

This curl is the *objet petit a* which condenses the impossible-deadly Thing, serving as its stand-in and thus enabling us to entertain a livable relationship with it, without being swallowed up by it. As Jewish children put it when they play gently aggressive games: 'Please, bite me, but not too hard . . .'. This is the difference between 'normal' sexual repression and fetishism: in 'normal' sexuality, we think that the detail-feature that serves as the *cause* of desire is just a secondary obstacle that prevents our direct access to the Thing – that is, we overlook its key role; while in fetishism we simply *make the cause of desire directly into our object of desire*: a fetishist in *Vertigo* would not care about Madeleine, but simply focus his desire directly on the lock of hair; a fetishist suitor would engage directly with the chaperone and forget about the lady herself, the official goal of his endeavours.

So there is always a gap between the object of desire itself and its cause, the mediating feature or element that makes this object desirable. What happens in melancholy is that we get *the object of desire deprived of its cause*. For the melancholic, the object is there, but what is missing is the specific intermediary feature that makes it desirable.[10] For that reason, there is always at least a trace of melancholy in every true love: in love, the object is not deprived of its cause; it is, rather, that the very *distance* between object and cause collapses. This, precisely, is what distinguishes *love* from *desire*: in desire, as we have just seen, cause is distinct from object; while in love, the two inexplicably *coincide* – I magically love the beloved one *for itself*, finding *in it* the very point *from which* I find it worthy of love. And – back to Marx – what if his mistake was also to assume that the *object* of desire (unconstrained expanding productivity) would remain even when it was deprived of the *cause* that propels it (surplus-value)?

3   Coke as *objet petit a*

What is crucial here from the psychoanalytic perspective is the link between the capitalist dynamics of surplus-value and the libidinal dynamics of surplus-enjoyment. Let us elaborate this point apropos of Coca-Cola as the ultimate capitalist merchandise and, as such, as surplus-enjoyment personified. It is no surprise that Coke was first introduced as a medicine – its strange taste does not seem to provide any particular satisfaction; it is not directly pleasing and endearing; however, it is precisely as such, as transcending any immediate use-value (unlike water, beer or wine, which definitely do quench our thirst or produce the desired effect of satisfied calm), that Coke functions as the direct embodiment of '*it*': of the pure surplus of enjoyment over standard satisfactions, of the mysterious and elusive X we are all after in our compulsive consumption of merchandise.

The unexpected result of this feature is not that, since Coke does not satisfy any concrete need, we drink it only as a supplement, after some other drink has satisfied our substantial need – rather, it is this very superfluous character that makes our thirst for Coke all the more insatiable: as Jacques-Alain Miller put it so succinctly, Coke has the paradoxical property that the more you drink the thirstier you get, the greater your need to drink more – with that strange, bitter-sweet taste, our thirst is never effectively quenched.[11] So, when, some years ago, the advertising slogan for Coke was 'Coke is *it*!', we should note its thorough ambiguity: 'that's it' precisely in so far as that's *never* actually *it*, precisely in so far as every satisfaction opens up a gap of 'I want *more*!'. The paradox, therefore, is that Coke is not an ordinary commodity whereby its use-value is transubstantiated into an expression of (or supplemented with) the auratic dimension of pure (exchange) Value, but a commodity whose very peculiar use-value is itself already a direct embodiment of the supra-sensible aura of the ineffable spiritual surplus, a commodity whose very material properties are already those of a commodity. This process is brought to its conclusion in the case of caffeine-free diet Coke – why? We drink Coke – or any drink – for two reasons: for its thirst-quenching or nutritional value, and for its taste. In the case of caffeine-free diet Coke, nutritional value is suspended and the caffeine, as the key ingredient of its taste, is also taken away – all that remains is a pure semblance, an artificial promise of a substance which never materialized. Is it not true that in this sense, in the case of caffeine-free diet Coke, we almost literally 'drink nothing in the guise of something'?

What we are implicitly referring to here is, of course, Nietzsche's classic opposition between 'wanting nothing' (in the sense of 'I don't want anything') and the nihilistic stance of actively wanting Nothingness itself; following Nietzsche's path, Lacan emphasized how in anorexia, the subject does not simply 'eat nothing' – rather, she or he actively wants to eat the Nothingness (the Void) that is itself the ultimate object-cause of desire. (The same goes for Ernst Kris's famous patient who felt guilty of theft, although he did not actually steal anything: what he *did* steal, again, was the Nothingness itself.) So – along the same lines, in the case of caffeine-free diet Coke, we *drink the Nothingness itself*, the pure semblance of a property that is in effect merely an envelope of a void.

This example brings home the inherent link between three notions: that of Marxist surplus-value, that of the Lacanian *objet petit a* as surplus-enjoyment (the concept that Lacan elaborated with direct reference to Marxian surplus-value), and the paradox of the superego, perceived long ago by Freud: the more Coke you drink, the thirstier you are; the more profit you make, the more you want; the more you obey the superego command, the guiltier

you are – in all three cases, the logic of balanced exchange is disturbed in favour of an excessive logic of 'the more you give (the
more you repay your debts), the more you owe' (or 'the more you
have what you long for, the more you lack, the greater your craving'; or – the consumerist version – 'the more you buy, the more
you have to spend'): that is to say, of the paradox which is the
very opposite of the paradox of love where, as Juliet put it in her
immortal words to Romeo, 'the more I give, the more I have'.
The key to this disturbance, of course, is the surplus-enjoyment,
the *object petit a*, which exists (or, rather, persists) in a kind of
curved space – the nearer you get to it, the more it eludes your
grasp (or the more you possess it, the greater the lack).[12]

Perhaps sexual difference comes in here in an unexpected
way: the reason why the superego is stronger in men than in
women is that it is men, not women, who are intensely related to
this excess of the surplus-enjoyment over the pacifying functioning of the symbolic Law. In terms of the paternal function,
the opposition between the pacifying symbolic Law and the
excessive superego injunction is, of course, the one between the
Name-of-the-Father (symbolic paternal authority) and the
'primordial father' who is allowed to enjoy all women; and it is
crucial here to recall that this rapist 'primordial father' is a male
(obsessional), not feminine (hysterical) fantasy: it is men who are
able to endure their integration into the symbolic order only
when this integration is sustained by some hidden reference to
the fantasy of the unbridled excessive enjoyment embodied in the
unconditional superego injunction to enjoy, to go to the extreme,
to transgress and constantly to force the limit. In short, it is men
in whom the integration into the symbolic order is sustained by
the superego exception.

This superego-paradox also allows us to throw a new light on to the functioning of today's artistic scene. Its basic feature is not only the much-deplored commodification of culture (art objects produced for the market), but also the less noted but perhaps even more crucial *opposite* movement: the growing *'culturalization' of the market economy itself*. With the shift towards the tertiary economy (services, cultural goods), culture is less and less a specific sphere exempted from the market, and more and more not just one of the spheres of the market, but its central component (from the software amusement industry to other media productions). What this short circuit between market and culture entails is the waning of the old modernist avant-garde logic of provocation, of shocking the establishment. Today, more and more, the cultural–economic apparatus itself, in order to reproduce itself in competitive market conditions, has not only to tolerate but directly to provoke stronger and stronger shocking effects and products. Just think of recent trends in the visual arts: gone are the days when we had simple statues or framed paintings – what we get now are exhibitions of frames without paintings, dead cows and their excrement, videos of the insides of the human body (gastroscopy and colonoscopy), the inclusion of olfactory effects, and so on.[13] Here again, as in the domain of sexuality, perversion is no longer subversive: such shocking excesses are part of the system itself; the system feeds on them in order to reproduce itself. Perhaps this is one possible definition of postmodern as opposed to modernist art: in postmodernism, the transgressive excess loses its shock value and is fully integrated into the established artistic market.[14]

Another way to make the same point would be to emphasize how, in today's art, the gap that separates the sacred space of sublime beauty from the excremental space of trash (leftover) is gradually narrowing, up to the paradoxical identity of opposites: are not modern art objects more and more excremental objects, trash (often in a quite literal sense: faeces, rotting corpses . . .) displayed in – made to occupy, to fill in – the sacred *place* of the Thing? And is not this identity in a way the hidden 'truth' of the entire movement? Is not every element that claims the right to occupy the sacred place of the Thing by definition an excremental object, a piece of trash that can never be 'up to its task'? This identity of opposite determinations (the elusive sublime object and/or excremental trash) – with the ever-present threat that the one will shift into the other, that the sublime Grail will reveal itself to be nothing but a piece of shit – is inscribed in the very kernel of the Lacanian *objet petit a*.

In its most radical dimension, this impasse is the impasse that affects the process of sublimation – not in the common sense that art production today is no longer able to generate properly 'sublime' objects, but in a much more radical sense: the very fundamental matrix of sublimation, that of the central Void, the empty ('sacred') place of the Thing exempted from the circuit of everyday economy, which is then filled in by a positive object that is thereby 'elevated to the dignity of the Thing' (Lacan's definition of sublimation), seems to be increasingly under threat; what is threatened is the very gap between the empty Place and the (positive) element filling it in. If, then, the problem of traditional (premodern) art was how to fill in the sublime Void of the Thing (the pure Place) with an adequately beautiful object – how to succeed in elevating an ordinary object to the dignity of a Thing – the problem of modern art is, in a way, the opposite (and much more desperate) one: one can no longer count on the Void of the (Sacred) Place being there, offering itself to be occupied by human artefacts, so the task is to sustain the Place as such, to make sure that this Place itself will 'take place' – in other words, the problem is no longer that of *horror vacui*, of filling in the Void, but, rather, that of *creating* the Void in the first place. Thus the co-dependence between an *empty, unoccupied place* and a rapidly moving, elusive object, an *occupant without a place*, is crucial.[15]

The point is not that there is simply the surplus of an element over the places available in the structure, or the surplus of a place that has no element to fill it out – an empty place in the structure would still sustain the fantasy of an element that will emerge and fill out this place; an excessive element lacking its place would still sustain the fantasy of an as yet unknown place waiting for it. The point is, rather, that the empty place in the structure is in itself *correlative* to the errant element lacking its place: they are not two different entities, but the obverse and reverse of one and the same entity – that is, one and the same entity inscribed into the two surfaces of a Moebius strip. In other words, the paradox is that *only an element which is thoroughly 'out of place'* (an excremental object, a piece of 'trash' or leftover) *can sustain the void of an empty place*, that is, the Mallarméan situation in which *rien n'aura eu lieu que le lieu* ('nothing but the place will have taken place') – the moment this excessive element 'finds its proper place', there is no longer any pure Place distinguished from the elements which fill it out.[16]

Another way to approach this tension between the Object and the Void would be through the different modalities of *suicide*. First there is, of course, suicide as an act that 'bears a message' (of protest against political, erotic, and so on, disappointment), and is, as such, addressed to the Other (for example, political suicides like public burnings which are supposed to shock and awaken the indifferent public). Although it involves the dimension of the Symbolic, this suicide is, at its most fundamental, *imaginary* – for the simple reason that the subject who accomplishes it is sustained in it by the *imagined* scene of the effect his or her act will have on posterity, on its witnesses, on the public, on those who will learn about it; the narcissistic satisfaction provided by such imagining is obvious. . . . Then there is suicide in the *Real*: the violent *passage à l'acte*, the subject's full and direct identification with the object. That is to say, for Lacan, the subject ($ – the 'barred', empty subject) and the object-cause of its desire (the leftover which embodies the lack that 'is' the subject) are strictly correlative: there is a subject only in so far as there is some material stain/leftover that *resists* subjectivization, a surplus in which, precisely, the subject *cannot* recognize itself. In other words, the paradox of the subject is that it exists only through its own radical impossibility, through a 'bone in the throat' that forever prevents it (the subject) from achieving its full ontological identity.

So we have here the structure of the Moebius strip: the subject is correlative to the object, but in a negative way – subject and object can never 'meet'; they are in the same place, but on opposite sides of the Moebius strip. Or – to put it in philosophical terms – subject and object are identical in the Hegelian sense of the speculative coincidence/identity of radical opposites: when Hegel praises the speculative truth of the vulgar materialist thesis of phrenology 'The Spirit is a bone', his point is not that the spirit can actually be reduced to the shape of the skull, but that there is a spirit (subject) only in so far as there is some bone (some inert material, non-spiritual remainder/leftover) that *resists* its spiritual sublation–appropriation–mediation. Subject and object are thus not simply external: the object is not the external limit with regard to which the subject defines its self-identity, it is ex-timate with regard to the subject, it is its *internal* limit – that is, the bar which itself prevents the subject's full realization.

What happens in the suicidal *passage à l'acte*, however, is precisely the subject's *direct* identification with the object: the object is no longer 'identical' to the subject in the sense of the Hegelian speculative identity of the dialectical process with the very obstacle that sustains this process – they coincide *directly*; they find themselves on the *same* side of the Moebius strip. This means that the subject is no longer the pure Void of negativity ($), the infinite desire, the Void in search of the absent object, but 'falls into' the object directly, becomes the object; and – vice versa – the object (cause of desire) is no longer the materialization of the Void, a spectral presence that merely gives body to the lack that sustains the subject's desire, but acquires a direct positive existence and ontological consistency. Or, to put it in the terms of the minimal gap between the Object and its Place, the Void/Clearing within which the object appears: what happens in the suicidal *passage à l'acte* is not that the object falls out of its frame, so that we get only the empty frame–void (i.e. so that 'nothing but the place itself takes place'); what happens, rather, is the exact opposite – the object is still there; it is the Void–Place that disappears; it is the frame that falls into what it frames, so that what occurs is the eclipse of the symbolic opening, the total closure of the Real. As such, not only is the suicidal *passage à l'acte* not the highest expression of the death drive; rather, it is the exact opposite of the death drive.

For Lacan, creative sublimation and the death drive are strictly correlative: the death drive empties the (sacred) Place, creates the Clearing, the Void, the Frame, which is then filled in by the object 'elevated to the dignity of the Thing'. Here we encounter the third kind of suicide: the 'suicide' that defines the death drive, *symbolic* suicide – not in the sense of 'not dying really, just symbolically', but in the more precise sense of the erasure of the symbolic network that defines the subject's identity, of cutting off all the links that anchor the subject in its symbolic substance. Here, the subject finds itself totally deprived of its symbolic identity, thrown into the 'night of the world' in which its only correlative is the minimum of an excremental leftover, a piece of trash, a mote of dust in the eye, an *almost-nothing* that sustains the pure Place–Frame–Void, so that here, finally, 'nothing but the place takes place'. So the logic of displaying an excremental object in the sublime Place is similar to the way the Hegelian infinite judgement 'The spirit is a bone' functions: our first reaction to Hegel's 'The spirit is a bone' is 'But this is senseless – spirit, its absolute, self-relating negativity, is the very *opposite* of the inertia of a skull, this dead object!' – however, this very awareness of the thorough incongruity between 'spirit' and 'bone' *is* the 'Spirit', its radical negativity. . . . Along the same lines, the first reaction to seeing faeces in the sublime Place is to ask indignantly: 'Is *this* art?' – but it is precisely this negative reaction, this experience of the radical incongruity between the object and the Place it occupies, that makes us aware of the specificity of this Place.

And, in effect, as Gérard Wajcman suggests in his remarkable book *L'objet du siècle*,[17] is not the great effort of modernist art focused on how to maintain the minimal structure of sublimation, the minimal gap between the Place and the element that fills it in? Is this not why Kasimir Malevich's 'Black Square on White Surface' expresses the artistic endeavour at its most elementary, reduced to the stark distinction between the Void (the white background/surface) and the element (the 'heavy' material stain of the square)? That is to say, we should always bear in mind that the very tense [*futur antérieur*] of Mallarmé's famous *rien n'aura eu lieu que le lieu* makes it clear that we are dealing with a utopian state which, for a priori structural reasons, can never be realized in the present tense (there will never be a present time in which 'only the place itself will take place'). It is not only that the Place it occupies confers sublime dignity on an object; it is also that only the presence of this object sustains the Void of the Sacred Place, so that the Place itself never *takes place*, but is always something which, retroactively, 'will have taken place' after it has been disturbed by a positive element. In other words, if we subtract from the Void the positive element, the 'little bit of reality', the excessive stain that disturbs its balance, we do not get the pure balanced Void 'as such' – rather, the Void itself disappears, is no longer there. So the reason why excrements are elevated into a work of art, used to fill in the Void of the Thing, is not simply to demonstrate that 'anything goes', that the object is ultimately irrelevant, since any object can be elevated into and occupy the Place of the Thing; this recourse to excrement, rather, bears witness to a desperate strategy to ascertain that the Sacred Place is still there.

The problem is that today, in the double movement of the progressive commodification of aesthetics and the aesthetification of the universe of commodities, a 'beautiful' (aesthetically pleasing) object is less and less able to sustain the Void of the

Thing – so it is as if, paradoxically, the only way to sustain the (Sacred) Place is to fill it up with trash, with an excremental abject. In other words, it is today's artists who display excremental objects as objects of art who, far from undermining the logic of sublimation, are desperately striving to *save* it. And the consequences of the collapse of the element into the Void of the Place itself are potentially catastrophic: without the minimal gap between the element and its Place, there simply is no symbolic order. That is to say, we dwell within the symbolic order only in so far as every presence appears against the background of its possible absence (this is what Lacan is aiming at with his notion of the phallic signifier as the signifier of castration: this signifier is the 'pure' signifier, the signifier 'as such', at its most elementary, in so far as its very presence stands for, evokes *its own* possible absence/lack).

Perhaps the most succinct definition of the modernist break in art is thus that, through it, the tension between the (art) Object and the Place it occupies is reflectively taken into account: what makes an object a work of art is not simply its direct material properties, but the place it occupies, the (sacred) Place of the Void of the Thing. In other words, with modernist art a certain innocence is lost for ever: we can no longer pretend that we directly produce objects which, on account of their properties – that is to say, independently of the place they occupy – 'are' works of art. For this reason, modernist art is forever split between the two extremes represented at its very origins by Malevich and Marcel Duchamp: on the one side the pure formal marking of the gap which separates the Object from its Place ('Black Square'); on the other, the display of a common everyday ready-made object (a bicycle) as a work of art, as if to prove that what constitutes art hinges not on the qualities of the art object but exclusively on the Place this object occupies, so that anything, even shit, can 'be' a work of art if it finds itself in the right Place. And whatever we do after the modernist break, even if it is the return to fake neoclassicism *à la* Arno Brekker, is already 'mediated' by that break.

Let us take a twentieth-century 'realist' like Edward Hopper: (at least) three features of his work bear witness to this mediation. First, Hopper's well-known tendency to paint city-dwellers at night, alone in an overlit room, seen from outside, through the frame of a window – even if the window framing the object is not there, the picture is drawn in such a way that the viewer is compelled to imagine an invisible immaterial frame separating him or her from the painted objects. Second, the way Hopper's pictures, in the very hyperrealist way they are drawn, produce in their viewer an effect of derealization, as if we are dealing with dreamy, spectral, aethereal things, not common material things (like the white grass in his countryside paintings). Third, the fact that his series of paintings of his wife sitting alone in a room illuminated by strong sunlight, staring through the open window, is experienced as an unbalanced fragment of a global scene, calling for a supplement, referring to an invisible off-space, like the still of a film shot without its counter-shot (and one can in fact maintain that Hopper's paintings are already 'mediated' by the cinematic experience).

In this precise sense, one is tempted to assert the contemporaneity of artistic modernism with Stalinism in politics: in the Stalinist elevation of the 'wise leader', the gap that separates the object from its place is also brought to an extreme and thus, in a way, reflectively taken into account. In his key essay 'On the

problem of the Beautiful in Soviet Art' (1950), the Soviet critic
G. Nedoshivin claimed:

> Amidst all the beautiful material of life, the first place should
> be occupied by images of our great leaders. . . . The sublime
> beauty of the leaders . . . is the basis for the coinciding of the
> 'beautiful' and the 'true' in the art of socialist realism.[18]

How are we to understand this logic which, ridiculous as it may
seem, is at work even today, with North Korea's Kim Yong Il?[19]
These characterizations do not refer to the Leader's actual properties – the logic here is the same as that of the Lady in courtly
love who, as Lacan emphasized, is addressed as an abstract Ideal,
so that 'writers have noted that all the poets seem to be address-
ing the same person. . . . In this poetic field the feminine object is
emptied of all real substance.'[20] This abstract character of the
Lady indicates the abstraction that pertains to a cold, distanced,
inhuman partner – the Lady is by no means a warm, compassionate, understanding fellow-creature:

> By means of a form of sublimation specific to art, poetic
> creation consists in positioning an object I can only describe
> as terrifying, an inhuman partner.
>
> The Lady is never characterized for any of her real,
> concrete virtues, for her wisdom, her prudence, or even her
> competence. If she is described as wise, it is only because she
> embodies an immaterial wisdom or because she represents
> its functions more than she exercises them. On the contrary,
> she is as arbitrary as possible in the tests she imposes on her
> servant.[21]

And is it not the same with the Stalinist Leader? Does he not, when he is hailed as sublime and wise, also 'represent these functions more than he exercises them'? Nobody would claim that Malenkov, Beria and Khrushchev were examples of male beauty – the point is simply that they 'represented' the function of beauty. . . . (In contrast to the Stalinist Leader, the psychoanalyst is *'objectively' ugly* even if he is actually a beautiful or sexually attractive person: in so far as he occupies the impossible place of the abject, of the excremental remainder of the symbolic order, he *'represents' the function of ugliness.*) In this sense, the designation of the Stalinist Leader as 'sublime' is to be taken literally, in the strict Lacanian sense: his celebrated wisdom, generosity, human warmth, and so on, are pure representations embodied by the Leader whom we 'can only describe as terrifying, an inhuman partner' – not symbolic authority obeying a Law, but a capricious Thing which is 'as arbitrary as possible in the tests it imposes on its servants'. Thus the price the Stalinist Leader pays for his elevation into the sublime object of beauty is his radical 'alienation': as with the Lady, the 'real person' is effectively treated as an appendage to the fetishized and celebrated public Image. No wonder the practice of retouching was so widely used in official photographs, with a clumsiness that is often so obvious that it is difficult to believe it was not intentional – as if to show that the 'real person', with all its idiosyncrasies, is to be totally replaced by its alienated wooden effigy. (One of the rumours about Kim Yong Il is that he actually died in a car crash a couple of years ago, and that in recent years a double has replaced him in his rare public appearances, so that the crowds can catch a glimpse of the object of their worship – is this not the best possible confirmation of the fact that the 'real personality' of the Stalinist Leader is thoroughly *irrelevant*, a replaceable object, since it does not matter if it is the 'real' Leader or his double, who has no actual power?) Is not this practice of elevating a common vulgar figure into the ideal of Beauty – of reducing beauty to a purely functional notion – strictly correlative to the modernist elevation of an 'ugly' everyday excremental object into a work of art?[22]

One of the most illuminating ways of locating this break between traditional and modern art would be via reference to the painting that in effect occupies the place of the 'vanishing mediator' between the two: Gustave Courbet's (in)famous 'L'origine du monde', the torso of a shamelessly exposed, headless, naked and aroused female body, focusing on her genitalia; this painting, which literally vanished for almost a hundred years, was finally – and quite appropriately – found among Lacan's belongings after his death.[23] 'L'origine' expresses the deadlock (or dead end) of traditional realist painting, whose ultimate object – never fully and directly shown, but always hinted at, present as a kind of underlying point of reference, starting at least from Albrecht Dürer's *Verweisung* – was, of course, the naked and thoroughly sexualized female body as the ultimate object of male desire and gaze. Here the exposed female body functioned in a way similar to the underlying reference to the sexual act in classic Hollywood movies, best described in the movie tycoon Monroe Stahr's famous instruction to his scriptwriters from Scott Fitzgerald's *The Last Tycoon*:

> At all times, at all moments when she is on the screen in our sight, she wants to sleep with Ken Willard. . . . Whatever she does, it is in place of sleeping with Ken Willard. If she walks down the street she is walking to sleep with Ken Willard, if

she eats her food it is to give her enough strength to sleep with Ken Willard. *But* at no time do you give the impression that she would even consider sleeping with Ken Willard unless they were properly sanctified.[24]

So the exposed female body is the impossible object which, precisely because it is unrepresentable, functions as the ultimate horizon of representation whose disclosure is forever postponed – in short, as the Lacanian incestuous Thing. Its absence, the Void of the Thing, is then filled in by 'sublimated' images of beautiful but not totally exposed female bodies – by bodies which always maintain a minimal distance towards That. But the crucial point (or, rather, the underlying illusion) of traditional painting is that the 'true' incestuous naked body is none the less waiting there to be discovered – in short, the illusion of traditional realism does not lie in the faithful rendering of the depicted objects; rather, it lies in the belief that *behind* the directly rendered objects *is* the absolute Thing which could be possessed if only we were able to discard the obstacles or prohibitions that prevent access to it.

What Courbet accomplishes here is the gesture of radical *desublimation*: he took the risk and simply went to the end by *directly depicting* what previous realistic art merely hinted at as its withdrawn point of reference – the outcome of this operation, of course, was (to put it in Kristevan terms) the reversal of the sublime object into abject, into an abhorrent, nauseating excremental piece of slime. (More precisely, Courbet masterfully continued to dwell on the imprecise border that separates the sublime from the excremental: the woman's body in 'L'origine' retains its full erotic attraction, yet it becomes repulsive precisely on account of this excessive attraction.) Courbet's gesture is thus a dead end, the dead end of traditional realist painting – but precisely as such, it is a necessary 'mediator' between traditional and modernist art – that is to say, it represents a gesture that *had to be accomplished* if we were to 'clear the ground' for the emergence of modernist 'abstract' art.

With Courbet, the game of referring to the forever absent 'realist' incestuous object is over, the structure of sublimation collapses, and the enterprise of modernism is to re-establish the matrix of sublimation (the minimal gap that separates the Void of the Thing from the object that fills it in) outside this 'realist' constraint, that is, outside the belief in the real presence of the incestuous Thing behind the deceptive surface of the painting. In other words, with Courbet, we learn that there is no Thing behind its sublime appearance – that if we force our way through the sublime appearance to the Thing itself, all we will get is a suffocating nausea of the abject; so the only way to re-establish the minimal structure of sublimation is directly to stage *the Void itself*, the Thing as the Void–Place–Frame, without the illusion that this Void is sustained by some hidden incestuous Object.[25] We can now understand in what precise way – and paradoxical as it may sound – Malevich's 'Black Square', as the seminal painting of modernism, is the true counterpoint to (or reversal of) 'L'origine': with Courbet, we get the incestuous Thing itself which threatens to implode the Clearing, the Void in which (sublime) objects (can) appear; while with Malevich, we get its exact opposite, the matrix of sublimation at its most elementary, reduced to the bare marking of the distance between foreground and background, between a wholly 'abstract' object (square) and the Place that contains it. The 'abstraction' of modernist painting should therefore be viewed as a reaction to the overt presence of the ultimate 'concrete' object, the incestuous Thing, which turns it into a disgusting abject – that is to say, turns the sublime into an excremental excess.[26]

And the task of historical materialist analysis here is to locate these all too formal determinations in their concrete historical context. First, of course, there is the aestheticization of the universe of commodities mentioned above: its ultimate result is that – to put it in somewhat pathetic terms – today, the true pieces of trash are the 'beautiful' objects with which we are constantly bombarded from all sides; consequently, the only way to escape trash is to put *trash itself* into the sacred place of the Void. However, the situation is more complex. On the one hand, there is the experience of (real or fantasized) global catastrophes (from nuclear or ecological catastrophe to holocaust) whose traumatic impact is so strong that they can no longer be conceived of as simple events that take place *within* the horizon/clearing sustained by the Void of the Thing – in them, the very Thing is no longer absent, that is, present as a Void, as the background of actual events, but threatens to become *directly* present, to actualize itself in reality, and thus to provoke a psychotic collapse of the symbolic space. On the other hand, the prospect of a global catastrophe was not peculiar to the twentieth century – so why did it have such an impact precisely in that century, and not before? Again, the answer lies in the progressive overlapping of aesthetics (the space of sublime beauty exempt from social exchange) and commodification (the very terrain of exchange): it is this overlapping and its result, the draining away of the very capacity to sublimate, that changes every encounter with the Thing into a disruptive global catastrophe, the 'end of the world'.

No wonder, then, that in the work of Andy Warhol, the ready-made everyday object that found itself occupying the sublime Place of a work of art was none other than a row of Coke bottles.

4   From *tragique* to *moque-comique*

The intersubjective consequences of this process are no less decisive. Because it is focused on the surplus of *objet petit a*, capitalism is no longer the domain of the discourse of the Master. This is where Lacan takes over and paraphrases in his own terms the old Marxian theme, from *The Manifesto*, of how capitalism dissolves all stable links and traditions; how, at its onslaught, 'all that is solid melts into air'. Marx himself made it clear that this 'all that is solid' does not concern only and primarily material products, but also the stability of the symbolic order that provides a definitive identification for subjects. So, on the one hand, instead of stable products destined to last for generations, capitalism introduces a breathtaking dynamics of obsolescence: we are bombarded by new and newer products which are sometimes obsolete even before they come fully into use – PCs have to be replaced every year if one is to keep up with the Joneses; long-playing records were followed by CDs, and now by DVDs. The aftermath of this constant innovation is, of course, the permanent production of piles of discarded waste:

> The main production of the modern and postmodern capitalist industry is precisely waste. We are postmodern beings because we realize that all our aesthetically appealing consumption artifacts will eventually end as leftover, to the point

that it will transform the earth into a vast waste land. You lose the sense of tragedy, you perceive progress as derisive.[27]

The obverse of the incessant capitalist drive to produce new and newer objects is therefore the growing pile of useless waste, mountains of used cars, computers, and so on, like the famous aeroplane 'resting place' in the Mojave desert. . . . In these ever-growing piles of inert, dysfunctional 'stuff', which cannot but strike us with their useless, inert presence, one can, as it were, perceive the capitalist drive at rest. That is the interest of Andrei Tarkovsky's films, most vividly his masterpiece *Stalker*, with its post-industrial wasteland: wild vegetation overgrowing abandoned factories, concrete tunnels and railroads full of stale water and wild overgrowth in which stray cats and dogs wander. Here again nature and industrial civilization overlap, but through a common decay – civilization in decay is again in the process of being reclaimed (not by idealized harmonious Nature, but) by nature in decomposition. The ultimate Tarkovskyan landscape is that of humid nature, a river or pool close to some forest, full of the debris of human artefacts (old concrete blocks or slabs of rusting metal). The ultimate irony of history is that it was a director from the Communist East who displayed the greatest sensitivity to this obverse of the drive to produce and consume. Perhaps, however, this irony displays a deeper necessity which hinges on what Heiner Müller called the 'waiting-room mentality' in Communist Eastern Europe:

There would be an announcement: The train will arrive at 18.15 and depart at 18.20 – and it never did arrive at 18.15. Then came the next announcement: The train will arrive at

20.10. And so on. You went on sitting there in the waiting room, thinking, It's bound to come at 20.15. That was the situation. Basically, a state of Messianic anticipation. There are constant announcements of the Messiah's impending arrival, and you know perfectly well that he won't be coming. And yet somehow, it's good to hear him announced all over again.[28]

The point of this Messianic attitude, however, was not that hope was maintained, but that since the Messiah did *not* arrive, people started to look around and take note of the inert materiality of their surroundings, in contrast to the West, where people, engaged in permanent frantic activity, do not even properly notice what is going on around them:

Because there was no acceleration in the culture, DDR citizens enjoyed more contact with the earth on which the waiting room was built; caught in this delay, they deeply experienced the idiosyncrasies of their world, all its topographical and historical details . . . while the delays in the East allowed people to accumulate experience, the imperative to travel forward destroyed any such potential in the West: if travel is a kind of death which renders the world banal, waiting engenders the accrual of substance.[29]

On the other hand – as the last sentence in the quote from Jacques-Alain Miller indicates – the same goes for interpersonal relations: Miller formulates this passage in terms of the shift from Master-Signifier to *objet petit a*: in the discourse of the Master, the subject's identity is guaranteed by S_1, by the Master-Signifier (his symbolic title–mandate), fidelity to which defines the subject's ethical dignity. Identification with the Master-Signifier leads to the tragic mode of existence: the subject endeavours to sustain his fidelity to the Master-Signifier – say, to the mission which gives meaning and consistency to his life – to the end, and his attempt ultimately fails because of the remainder that resists the Master-Signifier. In contrast, there is the slippery-shifting subject who lacks any stable support in the Master-Signifier, and whose consistency is sustained by relationship to the pure remainder/trash/excess, to some 'undignified', inherently comic, little bit of the Real; such an identification with the leftover, of course, introduces the mocking-comic mode of existence, the parodic process of the constant subversion of all firm symbolic identifications.

The exemplary case of this shift is the changed status of the Oedipal trajectory: what in Ancient Greece was still a pathetic tragedy, with the hero accomplishing the murderous act and then heroically assuming its consequences, turns in modernity into its own mocking parody. In his seminar on transference, Lacan refers to Claudel's Coûfontaine trilogy, in which the Oedipal parricide is given a comical twist: the son does shoot his father, but he misses, and the scared, undignified father simply dies of a heart attack. . . .[30] (Would it not be possible, in this precise sense, to claim that it was already *Oedipus at Colonus* which, with regard to *Oedipus the King*, was in a way the first example of the passage from *tragique* to *moque-comique*?) As Lacan indicates, however, this lack of tragedy proper paradoxically makes the modern condition even more horrifying: the fact is that in spite of all the horrors, from Gulag to Holocaust, from capitalism onwards there are no longer tragedies proper – the victims in concentration camps or the victims of the Stalinist show trials were not in a properly tragic predicament; their situation was not without comic – or, at least, ridiculous – aspects; and, for that reason, all the more horrifying – there is a horror so deep that it can no longer be 'sublimated' into tragic dignity, and is for that reason approachable only through an eerie parodic imitation/doubling of the parody itself.

Here, as in so many matters, it was Hegel who showed the way. That is to say, was it not Hegel who, in his famous sub-section on the 'world of self-alienated Spirit' in the *Phenomenology*, provided the definitive description of the passage from *tragique* to *moque-comique*, demonstrating how, in the process of dialectical mediation, every dignified, 'noble' position turns into its opposite – the truth of the 'noble consciousness' dedicated to its sublime ethical task of serving the Good is the manipulative, servile, exploitative 'base (knavish) consciousness':

> The content of what Spirit says about itself is thus the per-version of every Notion and reality, the universal deception of itself and others; and the shamelessness which gives utter-ance to this deception is just for that reason the greatest truth. This kind of talk is the madness of the musician 'who heaped up and mixed together thirty arias, Italian, French, tragic, comic, of every sort; now with a deep bass he descended into hell, then, contracting his throat, he rent the vaults of heaven with a falsetto tone, frantic and soothed, imperious and mocking, by turns.' (Diderot, *Nephew of Rameau*) To the tranquil consciousness which, in its honest way, takes the melody of the Good and the True to consist in the evenness of the notes, i.e. in unison, this talk appears as

a 'rigmarole of wisdom and folly, as a medley of as much skill as baseness, of as many correct as false ideas, a mixture compounded of a complete perversion of sentiment, of absolute shamefulness, and of perfect frankness and truth.' . . . This latter mind perverts in its speech all that is unequivocal, because what is self-identical is only an abstraction, but in its actual existence is in its own self a perversion.[31]

Two things about this remarkable passage should be emphasized. First, Marx's famous 'corrective' to Hegel's notion of historical repetition with which his *Eighteenth Brumaire* begins (history repeats itself, the first time as a tragedy, then as a farce) is already operative in Hegel himself: in his mad dance, Rameau's nephew *repeats* in a parodic way the *grandeur* of his uncle, the renowned composer, just as Napoleon III, the nephew, repeats in the mode of a farce the deeds of his uncle, *the* Napoleon. So it is already in Hegel that the two modes of repetition compete in a properly dialectical tension: the 'serious' repetition through which a historical contingency is 'sublated' into the expression of a historical necessity (Napoleon had to lose twice), and the 'comic' repetition that subverts the tragic identification. Secondly, we can see here clearly how the dialectical *passage* operates in Hegel – how we pass from In-itself to For-itself. Although the perverse speech of the 'nephew of Rameau' vocalizes the truth of the 'noble consciousness', his candid cynical admission of guilt none the less remains false – he is like a crook who thinks that he redeems himself by publicly acknowledging his crookedness (or, one is tempted to add, like a highly paid professor of Cultural Studies in Western academia who thinks that his incessant self-condemnatory critique of the

Eurocentrist, etc., bias of Western academia somehow exempts him from being implicated in it).

The guilt here concerns the tension between the subject of the statement and the subject of the enunciation (the subjective position *from which* one speaks): there is a way in which one can lie in the guise of (telling the) truth, that is, in which the full and candid admission of one's guilt is the ultimate deception, *the* way to preserve one's subjective position intact, free from guilt. In short, there is a way to *avoid* responsibility and/or guilt by, precisely, *emphasizing* one's responsibility or too readily *assuming* one's guilt in an exaggerated way, as in the case of the white male PC academic who emphasizes the guilt of racist phallogocentrism, and uses this admission of guilt as a stratagem *not* to face the way he, as a 'radical' intellectual, perfectly embodies the existing power relations towards which he pretends to be thoroughly critical. So – back to Diderot's *Rameau* – the problem with Rameau's nephew is not that his perverse negation of his dignified uncle's 'noble consciousness' is too radical and destructive, but that, in its very excess, it is *not radical enough*: the exaggerated perverse content which seems to explode the uncle's dignified speech is there to conceal the fact that, in both cases, the subjective position of enunciation *remains the same*. The more the admission is candid, inclusive of openly acknowledging the inconsistency of one's own position, the more it is false – in the same way, open confessions of the most intimate sexual, etc., details in today's talk shows really tell us *nothing* about the subject's inner truth (maybe because there is actually nothing to tell . . .).

To make the connection with the Marxist critique of political economy even clearer: for Hegel himself, this inherent subversion of noble consciousness finds its ultimate expression in *money*, a little, insignificant, piece of reality (metal) which possesses the magic power to invert every determination, no matter how noble and elevated, into its opposite, drawing it into a 'mad dance' which nothing can resist. No wonder Hegel conceives, as the speculative truth of this entire movement of the mediation of the 'noble consciousness', the infinite judgement 'The Self [*das Selbst*] is money [a piece of metal]', a new version of the infinite judgement of phrenology 'The Spirit is a bone'. In both cases, the dialectic of phrenology as well as the dialectic of wealth, the total 'liquefaction' of every firm determination, the disintegration of every determinate symbolic feature, culminates in its opposite: in the dialectical coincidence of pure subjectivity, of this power of the negative that dissolves every stable determination, with a meaningless, inert object, a leftover, trash (bone, money). One can now see what the Lacanian answer is to the Derridan insistence on how 'however it [the category of the subject] is modified, however it is endowed with consciousness or unconsciousness, it will refer, by the entire thread of its history, to the substantiality of a presence unperturbed by accidents, or to the identity of the proper/selfsame in the presence of self-relationship':[32] this 'substantiality' is not that of the subject itself, but that of its objectal counterpoint, of an excremental remainder/trash which precisely *sustains* the Subject *qua* empty/void/non-substantial. So we *do* have the empty, non-substantial subject – precisely as such, however, it has to be sustained by a minimum of a 'pathological' contingent objectal stain, *objet petit a*. This object is the paradoxical stand-in of the Void of subjectivity; it 'is' the subject itself in its otherness.

We all know Hegel's deservedly famous answer to Napoleon's

'No man is a hero to his valet': 'not, however, because the man is not a hero, but because the valet is a valet, whose dealings are with the man, not as a hero, but as one who eats, drinks, and wears clothes'[33] – in short, the valet's gaze is unable to perceive the world-historical dimension of the hero's public deeds. The lesson of the Lacanian *objet petit a* as the remainder of the Real here is that Hegel has to be supplemented: in order for the subjects to have a transferential relationship towards their hero, in order to venerate a person as a hero, the awareness of the world-historical dimension of his deeds is not enough; in order for this awareness to become a true veneration, it has to be supplemented by some detail from the 'pathological' domain of the hero's idiosyncratic fancies – it is only this 'little piece of reality', this touch of the 'real person' behind the public mask (some personal weakness or similar 'endearing foible'), that changes a noncommittal appreciation into true veneration. So for the hero to function effectively as a hero, the valet's intimate gaze has to support his public image – or, in Lacanese, the pathology of the *objet petit a* has to support S_1, the Master-Signifier, the symbolic mandate of the hero. And it is as if, today, this logic is brought to its self-destructive conclusion: it is no longer that we are simply interested in the private pathologies of public figures, or that public figures are directly *expected* to display signs of their 'common humanity' in public – the lesson of exhibitionist talk shows is that the very act of the public confession of their innermost private (sexual, etc.) idiosyncrasies *as such* can render a person famous, turning him or her into a public figure. . . .

Today, it is fashionable to search for one's 'true self' – Lacan's answer is that every subject is divided between *two* 'true Selves'. On the one hand, there is the Master-Signifier that delineates the contours of the subject's Ego-Ideal, his dignity, his mandate; on the other, there is the excremental leftover/trash of the symbolic process, some ridiculous detailed feature that sustains the subject's surplus-enjoyment – and the ultimate goal of psychoanalysis is to enable the subject–analysand to accomplish the passage from S_1 to *objet petit a* – to identify, in a kind of 'Thou Art That' experience, (with) the excremental remainder that secretly sustains the dignity of his symbolic identification. Consequently, this passage is the passage from *tragique* to *moque-comique* – with the important lesson that *objet petit a* is not simply sublime–elusive, but that, in it, the highest and the lowest coincide: *objet petit a* is precisely the zero-level of symbolic in-difference, the point at which the Holy Grail itself is revealed as nothing but a piece of shit. And it is crucial to note how this passage from symbolic identification to identification with the excremental leftover turns around – accomplishes in the opposite direction – the process of symbolic identification. That is to say, the ultimate paradox of the strict psychoanalytic notion of *symbolic* identification is that it is by definition a misidentification, the *identification with the way the Other(s) misperceive(s) me*. Let us take the most elementary example: as a father, I know I am an unprincipled weakling; but, at the same time, I do not want to disappoint my son, who sees in me what I am not: a person of dignity and strong principles, ready to take risks for a just cause – so I identify with this *misperception* of me, and truly 'become myself' when I, in effect, start to act according to this misperception (ashamed to appear to my son as I really am, I actually accomplish heroic acts). In other words, if we are to account for symbolic identification, it is not enough to refer to the opposition between the way I appear to others and the way I really am: symbolic identification occurs when the way

I appear to others becomes more important to me than the psychological reality 'beneath my social mask', forcing me to do things I would never be able to accomplish 'from within myself'.

How, then, are we to grasp the difference between the two gaps that characterize the symbolic process: the gap between the Master-Signifier and the series of 'ordinary' signifiers (S_1 and S_2), and the more radical gap between the very domain of the signifier (S) and its objectal remainder/leftover, *objet petit a*? There is an old racist joke, popular in ex-Yugoslavia, about a gipsy being examined by a psychiatrist. The psychiatrist first explains to the gipsy what free associations are: you immediately say what is on your mind in response to the psychiatrist's cue. Then the psychiatrist proceeds to the test itself: he says 'Table'; the gipsy answers: 'Fucking Fatima'; he says 'Sky'; the gipsy again answers: 'Fucking Fatima', and so on, until the psychiatrist explodes: 'But you didn't understand me! You must tell me what crops up in your mind, what you are thinking of, when I say my word!' The gipsy calmly answers: 'Yes, I got your point, I'm not that stupid, but I think *all the time* about fucking Fatima!'

This racist joke, which clearly displays the structure of Hegelian 'abstract universality', has none the less to be supplemented by the crucial final twist at work in another well-known joke about a pupil being examined by his biology teacher about different animals, and always reducing the answer to the definition of a horse: 'What is an elephant?' 'An animal which lives in the jungle, where there are no horses. A horse is a domestic mammal with four legs, used for riding, working in the fields or pulling vehicles.' 'What is a fish?' 'An animal which has no legs, unlike a horse. A horse is a domestic mammal . . .'. 'What is a dog?' 'An animal which, unlike horses, barks. A horse is a domestic mammal . . .' and so forth, until finally, the desperate teacher asks the pupil: 'OK, what is a *horse*?' Perplexed and totally thrown off balance, the poor surprised pupil starts to mumble and cry, unable to provide an answer. . . .

Along the same lines, the psychiatrist should have given the sex-starved gipsy the cue 'Fucking Fatima', at which, undoubtedly, the poor gipsy would have broken down in panic – even anxiety – unable to generate any association: why? Because, precisely (and in contrast to Bentham's theory of self-iconicity, according to which an object is the best icon of itself, that is, it resembles itself) a horse *is* a horse; it does not *look like* or *resemble* a horse; just as 'fucking Fatima' *is* 'fucking Fatima', not some association generated by the idea of 'fucking Fatima' – the Marx Brothers' well-known paradox 'No wonder you look like Emmanuel Ravelli, since you *are* Emmanuel Ravelli' involves an illegitimate short circuit. (Another homologous structure is that of a well-known tribe mentioned by Lévi-Strauss for whose members all dreams have a hidden sexual meaning – all, that is, *except* those with an explicit sexual content.)

To put it in philosophical terms, what we encounter here is the obverse of Leibniz's well-known principle according to which, if two things perfectly resemble each other, if all their properties are indistinguishable, they are also numerically identical – that is to say, one and the same thing: the anti-Leibnizean lesson of the Lacanian logic of the signifier is that since a thing does not 'look like itself', resemblance is, on the contrary, *the guarantor of non-identity*. (This paradox accounts for the uncanny effect of encountering a double: the more he looks like me, the more the abyss of his otherness is apparent.) Or, in Hegelese: the 'oneness' of a thing is grounded not in its properties, but in the negative synthesis of a pure 'One' which excludes (relates negatively to) all positive properties: this 'one' which guarantees the identity of a thing does not reside in its properties, since it is ultimately its *signifier*.

So here we have the difference between the series of ordinary signifiers and the central element ('horse', 'fucking Fatima') which has to remain empty in order to serve as the underlying organizing principle of the series. The homologous structure of the series and its exception underlies the figure of Kali, the Hindu goddess of destruction: she is usually portrayed as a terrifying, Medusa-like entity with dozens of limbs making aggressive gestures – however, as every Indian knows, the key point is that, among these limbs, a kind of meta-message is hidden, a tiny hand stretched out in a pacifying gesture, as if to say: 'Do not take all this ridiculous spectacle of horror too seriously! It is just a show of force, while in fact I am not really so menacing, but actually love you!' This exceptional sign is the one we have to look for in certain forms of aggressivity. . . .

Quite different from this gap that separates the exceptional Master-Signifier from the series of ordinary signifiers is the gap that separates the endless process of symbolic differentiation itself from the leftover that 'falls out' – the structure here is that of subdivision *ad infinitum* (in the sense of Hegelian 'spurious infinity') cut short by a sudden reversal. In mathematical terms, one could say that we reach the end when the two parts of the division are no longer two halves, parts of the previous element – when we no longer have a division between something and another (some)thing, but a division between something and *nothing* or, in terms of the logic of the signifier, a progressive diacritical division of signifiers reaches its end when we reach a division which is no longer the one between two signifiers of a signifying dyad, but a 'reflexive' division between the signifier *as such* with its *absence* – no longer between S_1 and S_2, but between S(ignifier) as such and $, the void, the lack of the signifier, which 'is' the (barred) subject itself. This 'bar' which is the subject means precisely that there is no signifier that can adequately represent it. And this is where the *object* comes in: what psychoanalysis calls the 'object' is precisely a phantasmic 'filler' that covers up this void of subjectivity, providing for it a semblance of being. This structure is perfectly expressed by a third joke, this time from today's Croatia, about President Franjo Tudjman.

Jokes about the Croatian President Franjo Tudjman in general display a structure of some interest for Lacanian theory – for example: Why is it impossible to play 'hide-and-seek' with Tudjman? Because if he were to hide, nobody would bother to seek him . . . a nice libidinal point about how hiding works only if people actually want to find you. But the supreme example is that of Tudjman and his large family in a plane above Croatia. Aware of the rumours that a lot of Croats lead miserable unhappy lives, while he and his cronies amass wealth, Tudjman says: 'What if I were to throw a cheque for a million dollars out of the window, to make at least one Croat, who will catch it, happy?' His flattering wife says: 'But Franjo, my dear, why don't you throw out two cheques for half a million each, and thus make two Croats happy?' His daughter adds: 'Why not four cheques for a quarter of a million each, and make four Croats happy?' and so on, until finally, his grandson – the proverbial innocent youth who unknowingly blurts out the truth – says: 'But Grandpa, why don't you simply throw yourself out of the window, and thus make *all* the Croats happy?' Here we have it all: the indefinite signifiers approach the impossible limit by subdividing, like Achilles trying to catch up with the tortoise, then this endless series caught in the logic of 'spurious infinity' is totalized, closed, completed, by the fall of the body whose Real stands for the subject himself. Through the suicidal fall of his body, the subject does not 'include himself out' but, on the contrary, totalizes the series by, as it were, *excluding himself in*. The body here is literally the 'indivisible remainder' that fills in the gap of the endless division.

5   Victims, Victims Everywhere

Postmodern deconstructionists would probably reject such a direct reference to the Real of the 'logic of Capital' as too 'essentialist', as not taking into account the radical openness and contingency of the struggle for hegemony. So what do we mean by it? Take the example of South Africa: of course, the end of apartheid was not directly conditioned by the objective 'logic of Capital', by Capital's universalism which tends to subvert and transgress all natural boundaries – it resulted from the heroic struggle of thousands of nameless freedom fighters. Nevertheless, as the current difficulties of the ANC government demonstrate, the end of apartheid confronted the black majority with their true dilemma: should they risk actually disturbing the free functioning of Capital in order to undo the effects of apartheid? Or should they make a pact with the Devil, and – like Clinton in the USA or New Labour in the UK – accept the basic depoliticization of the economy, and limit themselves to the struggle for cultural, ethnic, sexual, etc., rights? The struggle for hegemony within today's postmodern politics *does* have a limit: it encounters the Real when it touches the point of actually disturbing the free functioning of Capital.

The top censored story of 1998 was that of a secret international agreement called MAI (the Multilateral Agreement on Investment). The primary goal of MAI will be to protect the foreign interests of multinational companies. The agreement will basically undermine national sovereignty by assigning to these corporations powers almost equal to those of the countries in which they are located. Governments will no longer be able to treat their domestic firms more favourably than foreign firms. Furthermore, countries that do not relax their environmental, land-use, and health and labour regulations to meet the demands of foreign firms may be accused of acting illegally. Corporations will be able to sue sovereign states if they impose overstringent ecological or other standards – under NAFTA (the main model for MAI), Ethyl Corporation is already suing Canada for banning the use of its gasoline additive MMT. The greatest threat, of course, is to the developing nations, which will be pressured into depleting their natural resources for commercial exploitation. Renato Ruggerio, director of the World Trade Organization, the sponsor of MAI, is already hailing this project – elaborated and discussed in a clandestine manner, with almost no public consultation and media attention – as the 'constitution for a new global economy'.[34]

Just as for Marx, market relations provided the true foundation for the notion of individual freedoms and rights, *this* is the obverse of the much-praised new global morality celebrated even by some neoliberal philosophers as signalling the beginning of an era in which the international community will be able to enforce a minimal code preventing sovereign states from engaging in crimes against humanity even within their own territory. In a recent essay, significantly entitled 'Kosovo and the End of the Nation-State', Václav Havel tries to bring home the message that the NATO bombing of Yugoslavia:

> places human rights above the rights of the state. The Federal Republic of Yugoslavia was attacked by the alliance without a direct mandate from the UN. This did not happen irresponsibly, as an act of aggression or out of disrespect for international law. It happened, on the contrary, out of respect for the law, for a law that ranks higher than the law which protects the sovereignty of states. The alliance has acted out of respect for human rights, as both conscience and international legal documents dictate.[35]

Havel further specifies this 'higher law' when he claims that 'human rights, human freedoms, and human dignity have their deepest roots somewhere outside the perceptible world . . . while the state is a human creation, human beings are the creation of God'.[36] If we read Havel's two statements as the two premises of a judgement, the logical conclusion is none other than that NATO forces were allowed to violate existing international law, since they acted as a direct instrument of the 'higher law' of God Himself – if this is not a clear-cut case of 'religious fundamental-ism', then this term is devoid of any minimally consistent meaning.

Havel's statement is thus the strongest assertion of what Ulrich Beck, in an article in *Die Süddeutsche Zeitung* in April 1999, called 'militaristic humanism' or even 'militaristic pacifism'. The problem with this term is not that it is an Orwellian oxymoron – reminding us of 'Peace is war' and similar slogans from *Nineteen Eighty-Four* – which, as such, directly belies the truth of its position (against this obvious pacifist-liberal criticism, I rather think that it is the pacifist position – 'more bombs and killing never bring peace' – which is a fake, and that one should heroically *endorse* the paradox of militaristic pacifism). Neither is it that, obviously, the targets of a bombardment are not chosen out of pure moral consideration, but selectively, in accordance with unacknowledged geopolitical and economic strategic interests (the Marxist-style criticism). The problem is, rather, that this purely humanitarian-ethical legitimization (again) thoroughly *depoliticizes* the military intervention, changing it into an intervention in humanitarian catastrophe, grounded in purely moral reasons, not an intervention in a well-defined political struggle. In other words, *the problem with 'militaristic humanism/pacifism' lies not in 'militaristic' but in 'humanism/pacifism'*: in the way the 'militaristic' intervention (in the social struggle) is presented as help to the victims of (ethnic, etc.) hatred and violence, justified directly in depoliticized universal human rights. Consequently, what we need is not a 'true' (demilitarized) humanism/pacifism, but a 'militaristic' social intervention divested of its depoliticized humanist/pacifist veneer.

A report by Steven Erlanger on the suffering of the Kosovo Albanians in *The New York Times*[37] perfectly encapsulates this logic of victimization. Its title is revealing: 'In One Kosovo Woman, an Emblem of Suffering'; the subject to be protected (by NATO intervention) is identified from the outset as a powerless victim of circumstances, deprived of all political identity, reduced to stark suffering. Her basic stance is that of excessive suffering, of traumatic experience that blurs all differences: 'She's seen too much, Meli said. She wants a rest. She wants it to be over.' As such, she is beyond any political recrimination – an independent Kosovo is not on her agenda; she just wants the horror over: 'Does she favor an independent Kosovo? "You know, I don't care if it's this or that," Meli said. "I just want all this to end, and to feel good again, to feel good in my place and my house with my friends and family."' Her support of the foreign (NATO) intervention is grounded in her wish for all this horror to be over: 'She wants a settlement that brings foreigners here "with some force behind them." She is indifferent about who the foreigners are.' Consequently, she sympathizes with all sides in an all-embracing humanist stance: 'There is tragedy enough for everyone, she says. "I feel sorry for the Serbs who've been bombed and died, and I feel sorry for my own people. But maybe now there will be a conclusion, a settlement for good. That would be great."' Here we have the ideological construction of the ideal subject–victim in aid of whom NATO intervenes: not a political subject with a clear agenda, but a subject of helpless suffering, sympathizing with all suffering sides in the conflict, caught up in the madness of a local clash that can be pacified only by the intervention of a benevolent foreign power, a subject whose innermost desire is reduced to the almost animal craving to 'feel good again'. . . .

The ultimate paradox of the NATO bombing of Yugoslavia was thus not the one about which Western pacifists complained (by bombing Yugoslavia in order to prevent ethnic cleansing of Kosovo, NATO in effect triggered large-scale cleansing, and thus created the very humanitarian catastrophe it wanted to prevent), but a deeper paradox involved in the ideology of victimization:

the key aspect to note was NATO's privileging of the now-discredited 'moderate' Kosovar faction of Ibrahim Rugova against the 'radical' Kosovo Liberation Army. This means that NATO was actively blocking *the full-scale armed resistance of the Albanians themselves.* (The moment this option was mentioned, fears started to circulate: the KLA is not really an army, just a bunch of untrained fighters; we should not trust the KLA, since it is involved in drug-trafficking and/or is a Maoist group whose victory would lead to a Khmer Rouge or Taleban regime in Kosovo. . . .) After the agreement on the Serb Army's withdrawal from Kosovo, this distrust of the KLA resurfaced with a vengeance: the topic of the day was again the 'danger' that, after the Serb Army's withdrawal, the KLA would – as the NATO sources and the media liked to put it – 'fill the vacuum' and take over. The message of this distrust could not have been clearer: it's OK to help the *helpless* Albanians against the Serbian monsters, but in no way are they to be allowed actually to *cast off this help-lessness* by asserting themselves as a sovereign and self-reliant political subject, a subject with no need for the benevolent umbrella of the NATO 'protectorate'. . . .

In short, while NATO was intervening in order to protect the Kosovar victims, it was at the same time taking very good care that *they would remain victims*; inhabitants of a devastated country with a passive population, not an active politico-military force capable of defending itself. The NATO strategy was thus *perverse* in the precise Freudian sense of the term: it was itself (co-)responsible for the calamity against which it offered itself as a remedy (like the mad governess in Patricia Highsmith's *Heroine*, who sets the family house on fire in order to be able to prove her devotion to the family by bravely saving the children from the raging

flames . . .). What we encounter here is again the paradox of victimization: the Other to be protected is good *in so far as it remains a
victim* (which is why we were bombarded with pictures of helpless
Kosovar mothers, children and old people, telling moving stories
of their suffering); the moment it no longer behaves like a victim,
but wants to strike back on its own, it magically turns all of a
sudden into a terrorist/fundamentalist/drug-trafficking Other. . . .
The crucial point is thus to recognize clearly in this ideology of
global victimization, in this identification of the (human) subject
itself as 'something that can be hurt', the mode of ideology that fits
today's global capitalism. This ideology of victimization is the
very mode in which – most of the time invisible to the public eye,
and for that reason all the more ineluctable – the Real of Capital
exerts its rule.

On the other hand, the properly *uncanny* appeal of negative
gestures like the spectacular retreat of the German super-minis-
ter Oskar Lafontaine in some leftist circles also bears witness to
the same refusal to confront the Real of today's capitalism: the
very fact that he stepped down without giving reasons for his
action, combined with his demonization in the mass media (from
the front-page headline in *The Sun* – 'The most dangerous man in
Europe' – to the photo of him in *Bild*, showing him in profile, as
in a police photo after arrest), made him an ideal projection
screen for all the fantasies of the frustrated Left which rejects the
predominant Third Way politics. If Lafontaine were to stay, he
would save the essentials of the welfare state, restore the proper
role of the trade unions, reassert control over the 'autonomous'
financial politics of the state banks, even prevent the NATO
bombing of Yugoslavia. . . . While such an elevation of
Lafontaine into a cult figure has its positive side (it articulates the

utopian desire for an authentic Left that would break the hegemonic Third Way stance of accepting the unquestioned reign of
the logic of Capital), suspicions should none the less be raised
that there is something false about it: to put it in very simple
terms, if Lafontaine were actually in a position to accomplish at
least *some* of these goals, he would quite simply *not* step down, but
go on with his job. The cult of Lafontaine is thus possible only as
a negative gesture: it was his *stepping down* that created the void in
which utopian leftist energies could be invested, relying on the
illusion that if external circumstances (Schröder's opportunism,
etc.) were not preventing Lafontaine from doing his job, he
would actually accomplish something. The true problem, however, is: *what would have happened if Lafontaine had not been forced to step
down?* The sad but most probable answer is: either *nothing* of real
substance (i.e. he would have been gradually 'gentrified', co-
opted into the predominant Third Way politics, as had already
happened with Lionel Jospin in France), or his interventions
would have triggered a global economico-political crisis forcing
him, again, to step down, and discrediting Social Democracy as
unable to govern.[38]

The deadlock of globalization is felt most strongly in countries
like Russia, which, as it were, got the worst of both worlds:
Communist 'totalitarianism' as well as capitalist liberalism. Back
in the 1940s, Theodor Adorno pointed out how, in the late capitalist 'administered world', the classical Freudian notion of the
ego as the mediating agency between the two extremes, the inner
drives of the id and the external social constraints of the superego, is no longer operative: what we encounter in today's
so-called narcissistic personality is a direct pact between superego and id at the expense of the ego. The basic lesson of the

so-called 'totalitarianisms' is that the social powers represented in superego pressure directly manipulate the subject's obscene drives, bypassing the autonomous rational agency of the ego. Along the same lines, it is misleading to read today's Russian situation as one in which a proper balance must be struck between the two extremes: the Communist legacy of social solidarity, and the cruel game of open-market competition: the key feature of the Russian post-Communist situation is a direct pact (coincidence, even) between the darkest remainders of the past (secret KGB funds) and the most ruthless of the new capitalists – the emblematic figure of today's Russia is an ex-KGB apparatchik turned private banker with shady underground connections. . . .

According to the media, when – at a recent meeting of the leaders of the great Western powers, dedicated to the politico-ideological notion of the 'Third Way' – the Italian Prime Minister Massimo d'Alema said that one should not be afraid of the word 'socialism', Clinton – and, following him, Blair and Schröder – could not restrain themselves, and openly burst out laughing. This anecdote tells us a lot about the problematic character of today's talk about the Third Way. Crucial here is the curious enigma of the second way: where is the *second* way today? That is to say: did not the notion of the Third Way emerge at the very moment when – at least in the developed West – all other alternatives, from true conservativism to radical Social Democracy, lost out in the face of the triumphant onslaught of global capitalism and its notion of liberal democracy? Is not the true message of the notion of the Third Way therefore simply that *there is no second way*, no actual *alternative* to global capitalism, so that, in a kind of mocking pseudo-Hegelian negation of negation, this much-praised 'Third Way' brings us back to the *first and only* way – the Third Way is simply *global capitalism with a human face*, that is, an attempt to minimize the human costs of the global capitalist machinery, whose functioning is left undisturbed.

6 The Fantasmatic Real

Is, however, this fantasmatic spectrality – as opposed to social reality – actually identical to the (Lacanian) Real? Eric Santner's discussion of the Freudian figure of Moses provides an excellent description of the way spectrality operates in ideology:[39] what is in fact traumatic about this figure – about the Jewish break with the pagan pre-monotheistic cosmo-religion of One Nature in which a multitude of deities can coexist – is not simply the monotheistic repression of pagan enjoyment (sacred orgies, images . . .), but the excessively violent nature of the very gesture of repressing the pagan universe and imposing the universal rule of the One of Law. In other words, the 'repressed' of Jewish monotheism is *not* the wealth of pagan sacred orgies and deities but the disavowed excessive nature of *its own* fundamental gesture: that is – to use the standard terms – the crime that founds the rule of the Law itself, the violent gesture that brings about a regime which retroactively makes this gesture itself illegal/criminal. Santner refers here to the well-known paradox of 'there are no cannibals in our tribe, we ate the last one yesterday', conceiving Moses as the exemplary figure of such a last cannibal abolishing the condition of cannibalism (and, in contrast, the figure of Jesus as the last meal, the last victim to be slaughtered and eaten – following René Girard, who has conceived Christ's crucifixion as the sacrifice to end all sacrifices).[40]

Consequently, one should distinguish between *symbolic history* (the set of explicit mythical narratives and ideologico-ethical pre-scriptions that constitute the tradition of a community – what Hegel would have called its 'ethical substance') and its obscene Other, the unacknowledgeable *'spectral'*, *fantasmatic history* that effec-tively sustains the explicit symbolic tradition, but has to remain foreclosed if it is to be operative. What Freud endeavours to reconstitute in *Moses and Monotheism*[41] (the story of the murder of Moses, etc.) is such a spectral history that haunts the space of Jewish religious tradition. Santner uses a very precise formu-lation which immediately recalls Lacan's definition of the Real as Impossible from his Seminar *Encore*: the spectral fantasmatic history tells the story of a traumatic event that 'continues not to take place',[42] that cannot be inscribed into the very symbolic space it brought about by its intervention – as Lacan would have put it, the spectral traumatic event 'ne cesse pas de ne pas s'écrire', doesn't stop [or cease] *not* being written [*not* to inscribe itself]'[43] (and, of course, precisely as such, as nonexistent, it continues to persist; that is, its spectral presence continues to haunt the living).

One becomes a full member of a community not simply by identifying with its explicit symbolic tradition, but when one also assumes the spectral dimension that sustains this tradition: the undead ghosts that haunt the living, the secret history of trau-matic fantasies transmitted 'between the lines', through its lacks and distortions. In the Jewish tradition, there is a well-known story of a rabbi narrating to a young pupil the legend of a prophet to whom a Divine vision appeared; when the youngster eagerly asks him: 'Is this true? Did it really happen?', the rabbi answers: 'It probably didn't really happen, but it *is* true.'[44] In the same way, the murder of the primordial father and other

Freudian myths are in a way *more real than reality*: they are 'true', although, of course, they 'didn't really take place' – their spectral presence sustains the explicit symbolic tradition. Referring to Ian Hacking's recent work,[45] Santner draws a fine line of separation from the standard notion of the change in the narrative network which allows us to tell the coherent story of our past: when one changes from one narrative register to another that in a way allows us to 'rewrite the past', the emergence of the new 'descriptive vocabulary' has to foreclose/repress the traumatic excess of its own violent imposition, the 'vanishing mediator' between the old discursive regime and the new; and this 'vanishing mediator', precisely in so far as it remains non-integrated, excluded, continues to haunt 'actual' history as its spectral Other Scene. This foreclosed ('primordially repressed') myth that grounds the rule of *logos* is thus not simply a past event but a permanent spectral presence, an undead ghost that has to persist all the time if the present symbolic frame is to remain operative.

One should not confound this 'primordially repressed' myth (this 'fundamental fantasy') with the multitude of inconsistent daydreams that always accompany our symbolic commitments, allowing us to endure them. Let us recall the example of a ('straight') sexual relationship. The success of Peter Hoeg's *The Woman and the Ape* indicates that sex with an animal is today's predominant form of the fantasy of full sexual relationship, and it is crucial that this animal is as a rule male: in contrast to cyborg-sex fantasy, in which the cyborg is, as a rule, a woman (*Blade Runner*) – that is, in which the fantasy is that of Woman-Machine – the animal is a male ape copulating with a human woman, and fully satisfying her. Does this not materialize two standard common daydreams: that of a woman who wants a strong animal partner, a potent 'beast', not a hysterical impotent weakling; and that of a man who wants his female partner to be a perfectly programmed 'doll' who fulfils all his wishes, not a living being? What we should do in order to penetrate the underlying 'fundamental fantasy' is to stage these two fantasies together: to confront ourselves with the *unbearable ideal couple of a male ape copulating with a female cyborg*, the fantasmatic support of the 'normal' couple of man and woman copulating. The need for this redoubling, the need for this fantasmatic supplement to accompany the 'straight' sexual act as a spectral shadow, is yet another proof that 'there is no sexual relationship'.

Do we not find something quite similar in the superb final scene of *My Best Friend's Wedding*, when, at the wedding of Cameron Diaz, Julia Roberts (her 'best friend' who, throughout the film, has been trying to abort this wedding in order to win the bridegroom, her ex-boyfriend, back), resigned to the loss of her ex-partner, accepts the proposal of Rupert Everett, her close gay friend, and performs a passionate dance act with him in front of all the wedding guests: *they* are the true couple, to be opposed to the 'official' real couple of Cameron Diaz and her bridegroom, engaged in a full 'straight' sexual relationship. What is crucial here is that Julia Roberts and Rupert Everett, in contrast to this actual couple, are not engaged in sex: although they just put on a spectacle, although they are engaged in *performing a fake appearance*, it is precisely as such that their performance is in a way *more real* than the common reality of the 'actual sex' of the other couple. In short, this dance is *sublime* in the strict Kantian sense: what the two of them stage, what appears – *shines through* – their act is the fantasy, the impossible utopian dream, of the ultimate 'perfect couple' that the other 'actual' couple will never be able to come close to. . . . So, again, the gesture of Roberts and Everett is to stage the impossible fantasy whose spectre accompanies and redoubles the 'true' couple engaged in 'actual' sex – and the paradox is that they can do it precisely in so far as they are not an 'actual couple', precisely in so far as (because of their different sexual orientations) their relationship can never be consummated.

The lesson of all this is that, in the opposition between fantasy and reality, the Real is on the side of fantasy. Nowhere is this clearer than in the standard Hollywood procedure, under the pressure of the Hayes Code censorship rules, of retroactively transposing the main narrative into a nightmarish dream, so that at the end of the film, when the catastrophe is at its peak, we return to 'normal' everyday reality. To avoid the standard examples (from Robert Wiene's *Dr. Caligari* to Fritz Lang's *Woman in the Window*), let us turn to Robert Siodmak's *The Strange Affair of Uncle Harry* (1945): in the online *All-Movie Guide*, this film is qualified as 'OK for Children' but the 'keywords' used to characterize its plot are 'incest, kill, romance, schemer, sister' – an excellent example of how the 'innocent' reading can coexist with much more unsettling undertones.

Even more than *Woman in the Window*, *Uncle Harry* plays on the paradoxes of desire and its realization. John Quincy, an unmarried middle-aged fabric designer (played, in a superb case of anti-casting, by the sinister George Sanders) lives a dull life with his two domineering unmarried sisters, the older Hester and the younger Lettie, who look after him in their family manor in New Hampshire. He meets Deborah Brown, a visiting fashion expert from New York City; soon their friendship becomes love, and he asks her to marry him. When Deborah meets John's family, and

the sisters are informed of their plan to marry, Hester is happy
for her brother, while Lettie is violently jealous and feigns a heart
attack. Frustrated and angry at Lettie's attempt to spoil his happiness, John plans to murder her by poisoning her regular drink;
through a mistake, however, it is Hester who drinks the cup
intended for Lettie, and dies. Although she is aware that the
poison was for her, Lettie assumes the guilt and is condemned to
death for her sister's murder – although John publicly protests
that he did the poisoning, she refuses to corroborate his self-
incrimination, because she knows that her death will prevent
him from marrying Deborah. She tells him: 'I'll give you what
you always wanted, your freedom from me!', aware that in this
way she will make him indebted to her for ever, since he will owe
his freedom to her – by taking the guilt upon herself, and letting
him live, she changes the rest of his life into the vegetation of a
living dead. In short, Lettie takes his desire (to kill her) upon
herself, and thus frustrates him by fulfilling it. At the very end of
the film, John wakes up and discovers that the entire catastrophic situation of his poisoning his sister has been his dream:
what awakens him is the returning Deborah, and he merrily
elopes with her to New York, leaving his two sisters behind.

The paradox, of course, is that this very fictionalization of the
murder, to mollify the censors, introduces an additional element
of pathology – the film's final lesson is that 'the most disturbed
psyche in the film may actually have been that of the protago-
nist':[46] does not the fact that instead of simply confronting his
sister like a mature adult, he dreams of an elaborate poisoning
scheme, reveal his 'profound guilt over his sexual attraction to
her'?[47] The retroactive fictionalization *engages* the subject who
generated this fiction much more fundamentally than if he were

really to poison his sister: if we were dealing with a 'real-life' murder case, John would ultimately have been the victim of some externally imposed situation (of the unfortunate fact of having a domineering and possessive sister) – that is, it would have been possible for him (and us, spectators) to put the blame on circumstances; while the fictionalization of the murder attempt anchors the narrative events much more strongly in John's own libidinal tendencies. In other words, is not the underlying premiss of this fictionalization that John himself sustains the privileged intimate relationship with Lettie – that Lettie's dominant role satisfies John's own libidinal needs, and that his aggressive acting-out (his attempt to murder her) is also directed at the Real of his own unacknowledged 'passionate attachment'?[48] Did he not dream about his murderous act in order to avoid the 'happy' prospect, rejected by his unconscious, of abandoning the incestuous link with Lettie and marrying Deborah? When, at the end, he wakes up, he does so in order to escape the horrible prospect of the realization of his desire in all its fundamental ambiguity, since this realization implies that the fundamental 'passionate attachment' that structured his life is undone . . . (he gets rid of the obstacle, and is simultaneously even more indebted to his sister).

7   Why is the Truth Monstrous?

So what about the ghosts which are not to be simply dismissed as fantasmatic, since they haunt us on account of their very excessive, unbearable *reality*, like the Holocaust? Although this event set in motion the entire contemporary ethical discussion, it continues to haunt us as a spectral entity that cannot be fully 'accounted for', integrated into our social reality, even if we know (almost) all about it on the level of historical facts. Here, however, are we not confusing two different modalities of the trauma that is impossible to integrate into our symbolic universe: the fantasmatic narrative of a spectral event that definitely 'did not really happen' (like the Freudian myth of the primordial parricide) and the traces of an event that definitely *did* happen, but was too traumatic to be integrated into historical memory (like the Holocaust), so that we cannot register it as neutral, 'objective' observers, and accept it as part of our (past) reality – there is something 'spectral' about it not because its status is fantasmatic, but because of its very *excess* of reality? So it is crucial to distinguish here between the fantasmatic spectral narrative and the Real itself: one should never forget that the foreclosed traumatic narrative of the crime/transgression comes, as it were, after the (f)act; that it is in itself a lure, a 'primordial lie' destined to deceive the subject by providing the fantasmatic foundation of his or her being.

With regard to this point, one can precisely define the mystification of the theosophical mythopoeic narrative which claims to recount the genesis of the cosmos (of fully constituted reality, ruled by *logos*) out of proto-cosmic pre-ontological chaos. Such attempts obfuscate the point that the repressed spectral 'virtual history' is not the 'truth' of the official public history, but the fantasy which fills in the void of the *act* that brought history about.

On the level of family life, this distinction is palpable in so-called False Memory Syndrome: the 'memories' unearthed (being seduced/abused by the father), the repressed stories that haunt the imagination of the living, are precisely such 'primordial lies' destined to forestall the encounter with the ultimate rock of impossibility, the fact that 'there is no sexual relationship'. And the same goes, on the level of social life, for the notion of the primordial Crime that grounds the legal Order: the secret narrative that tells its story is purely fantasmatic. In philosophy proper, this fantasmatic mystification is at the very core of Schelling's *Weltalter* project.[49]

What Schelling endeavoured to accomplish in *Weltalter* is precisely such a mythopoeic fantasmatic narrative that would account for the emergence of *logos* itself out of the pre-logical proto-cosmic Real; however, at the very end of each of the three successive drafts of *Weltalter* – that is to say, at the very point at which the passage from *mythos* to *logos*, from the Real to the Symbolic, should have been deployed – Schelling was compelled to posit an uncanny *act* of *Ent-Scheidung*, an act that was in a way more primordial than the Real of the 'eternal Past' itself. So the repeated failure of his three successive *Weltalter* drafts indicates precisely Schelling's honesty as a thinker: the fact that he was radical enough to acknowledge the impossibility of grounding the act/decision in the proto-cosmic myth. The line of separation between materialism and obscurantist idealism in Schelling thus concerns precisely the relationship between act and proto-cosmos: idealist obscurantism deduces/generates the act from proto-cosmos, while materialism asserts the primacy of the act, and denounces the fantasmatic character of the proto-cosmic narrative.

That is to say: apropos of Schelling's claim that man's consciousness arises from the primordial act which separates present-actual consciousness from the spectral, shadowy realm of the Unconscious, one has to ask a seemingly naïve, but crucial question: what, precisely, is the Unconscious here? Schelling's answer is unequivocal: the 'Unconscious' is not primarily the rotary motion of drives ejected into the eternal past; the 'Unconscious' is, rather, the very act of *Ent-Scheidung* by means of which drives were ejected into the past. Or – to put it in slightly different terms – what is truly 'unconscious' in man is not the immediate opposite of consciousness, the obscure and confused 'irrational' vortex of drives, but the very founding gesture of consciousness, the act of decision by means of which I 'choose myself', that is, combine this multitude of drives into the unity of my Self. The 'Unconscious' is not the passive stuff of inert drives to be used by the creative 'synthetic' activity of the conscious ego; the 'Unconscious' in its most radical dimension is, rather, *the highest Deed of my self-positing*, or – to resort to later 'existentialist' terms – the choice of my fundamental 'project' which, in order to remain operative, must be 'repressed', kept unconscious, out of the light of day; or, to quote from the admirable last pages of the second draft of *Weltalter*:

The deed, once accomplished, sinks immediately into the unfathomable depth, thereby acquiring its lasting character. It is the same with the will which, once posited at the beginning and led into the outside, immediately has to sink into the unconscious. This is the only way the beginning, the beginning that does not cease to be one, the truly eternal beginning, is possible. For here also it holds that the beginning should not know itself. Once done, the deed is eternally done. The decision that is in any way the true beginning should not appear before consciousness, it should not be recalled to mind, since this, precisely, would amount to its recall. He who, apropos of a decision, reserves for himself the right to drag it again to light, will never accomplish the beginning.[50]

What we encounter here is, of course, the logic of the 'vanishing mediator': of the founding gesture of differentiation which must sink into invisibility once the difference between the 'irrational' vortex of drives and the universe of *logos* is in place. Schelling's fundamental move is thus not simply to ground the ontologically structured universe of *logos* in the horrible vortex of the Real; if we read him carefully, there is a premonition in his work that this terrifying vortex of the pre-ontological Real itself is (accessible to us only in the guise of) a fantasmatic narrative, a lure destined to distract us from the true traumatic cut, that of the abyssal act of *Ent-Scheidung*. And today this lesson is more relevant than ever: when we are confronted with an image of that deep horror which underlies our well-ordered surface, we should never forget that the images of this horrible vortex are ultimately a lure, a trap to make us forget where the true horror lies.

Let us clarify this crucial point with a perhaps unexpected example of two recent films, Roberto Benigni's *Life is Beautiful* and Thomas Vinterberg's *Celebration*. In Benigni, we have a father who assumes an almost maternal protective role, a father who relies on pure appearance, weaving for his son a protective web of fictions, a kind of ersatz-placebo; while Vinterberg presents the paternal figure as the monstrous rapist of his children – here, the obscene father, far from protecting the children from trauma, is the very cause of the trauma, the brutal *jouisseur*. . . . It is crucial here to avoid the trap of conceiving these two opposed poles (Benigni's protective father and Vinterberg's obscene father) along the axis of appearance versus reality: as if the opposition is that of pure appearance (the protective maternal father) versus the Real of the violent rapist that becomes visible once we tear down the false appearance. *Celebration* tells us a lot about how today, with False Memory Syndrome (of being abused by one's parents), the spectral figure of the Freudian *Urvater*, sexually possessing everyone around him, is resuscitated – it tells us a lot precisely on account of its artificial and fake character. That is to say: a simple sensitive look at *Celebration* tells us that there is something wrong and faked about all this pseudo-Freudian stuff about 'demystifying bourgeois paternal authority', revealing its obscene underside: today, such a 'demystification' sounds and is false; it functions more and more as an expression of nostalgia for the good old times in which it was still possible really to experience such 'traumas'. Why? We are not dealing here with the opposition between the appearance (of a benevolent, protective father) and the cruel reality (of the brutal rapist) that becomes visible once we demystify the appearance; on the contrary, it is this horrible secret of a brutal father behind the polite mask which is itself a fantasmatic construction.

The recent impasse around Binjamin Wilkomirski's *Fragments*[51] points in the same direction: what everyone assumed to be the blurred but authentic memories of the author who, as a three- to four-year-old child, was imprisoned in Majdanek, turned out to be a literary fiction invented by the author. Apart from the standard question of literary manipulation, are we aware how widely this 'fake' revealing of the fantasmatic investment and *jouissance* is operative in even the most painful and extreme conditions? That is to say, the enigma is as follows: usually, we generate fantasies as a kind of shield to protect us from the unbearable trauma; here, however, the very ultimate traumatic experience, that of the Holocaust, is fantasized as a shield – from what? Such monstrous apparitions are 'returns in the Real' of the failed symbolic authority: the reverse of the decline of paternal authority, of the father as the embodiment of the symbolic Law, is the emergence of the rapist, enjoying father of False Memory Syndrome. This figure of the obscene rapist father, far from being the Real beneath the respectable appearance, is, rather, itself a fantasy-formation, a protective shield – against what? Is the rapist father of False Memory Syndrome not, despite its horrifying features, the ultimate guarantee that *somewhere there is full, unconstrained enjoyment*? So what if the true horror is the lack of enjoyment itself?

What these two fathers (Benigni's and Vinterberg's) have in common is that they both *suspend the agency of the symbolic Law/Prohibition* – the paternal agency whose function is to introduce the child into the universe of social reality, with its harsh demands, to which the child is exposed without any maternal protective shield: Benigni's father offers the imaginary shield against the traumatic encounter with social reality, while Vinterberg's rapist father is also a father *outside the constraints of the (symbolic) Law*, enjoying access to full enjoyment. These two fathers thus fit the Lacanian opposition between the Imaginary and the Real: Benigni's is a protector of imaginary safety against the brutality of the Real of lawless violence – what is missing is the father as the bearer of symbolic authority, the Name-of-the-Father, the prohibitory 'castrating' agency that enables the subject's entry into the symbolic order, and thus into the domain of *desire*. The two fathers, imaginary and real, are what is left over once paternal symbolic authority disintegrates.

So what happens to the functioning of the symbolic order when the symbolic Law loses its efficiency, when it no longer functions properly? What we get are subjects who are strangely derealized or, rather, depsychologized, as if we are dealing with robotic puppets obeying a strange blind mechanism, rather like the way they are shooting soap operas in Mexico: because of the extremely tight schedule (the studio has to produce a half-hour instalment of the series every day), actors do not have time to learn their lines in advance, so they have a tiny voice receiver hidden in their ears, and a man in the cabin behind the set simply reads them their instructions (what words they are to say, what acts they are to perform) – actors are trained to enact these instructions immediately, with no delay. . . .

Another example from war can help us to clarify this point further. The ultimate lesson of the latest American military interventions, especially Operation Desert Fox against Iraq at the end of 1998, is that such operations signal a new era in military history – battles in which the attacking force operates under the constraint that it can sustain no casualties. (The same point is repeated in every US discussion about military intervention abroad, from Somalia to ex-Yugoslavia – one expects a guarantee that there will be no casualties.) This tendency to erase death itself from war should not, however, seduce us into endorsing the standard notion that war is rendered less traumatic if it is no longer experienced by the soldiers (or presented) as an actual encounter with another human being to be killed, but as an abstract activity in front of a screen or behind a gun far from the explosion, like guiding a missile on a warship hundreds of miles away from where it will hit its target.

While such a procedure makes the soldier less *guilty*, it is open to question if it actually causes less *anxiety* – this is one way to explain the strange fact that soldiers often fantasize about killing the enemy soldier in a face-to-face confrontation, looking him in the eyes before stabbing him with a bayonet (in a kind of military version of the sexual False Memory Syndrome, they even often 'remember' such encounters when they never in fact took place). There is a long literary tradition of elevating such face-to-face encounters as an authentic war experience (see the writings of Ernst Jünger, who praised them in his memoirs of the trench attacks in World War I). So what if the truly traumatic feature is *not* the awareness that I am killing another human being (to be obliterated through the 'dehumanization' and 'objectivization' of war into a technical procedure) but, on the contrary, this very 'objectivization', which then generates the need to supplement it by fantasies of authentic personal encounters with the enemy? It is thus not the fantasy of a purely aseptic war run as a video game behind computer screens that protects us from the reality of the face-to-face killing of another person; on the contrary, it is this fantasy of a face-to-face encounter with an enemy killed bloodily that we construct in order to escape the Real of the depersonalized war turned into an anonymous technological operation.

So our thesis should be clear now: the cruel reality of war relates to the notion of the virtualized war with no casualties in precisely the same way as *Festen* relates to Benigni's *Life is Beautiful*: in both cases, we are *not* dealing with the symbolic fiction (of virtual bloodless warfare, of protective narrative) concealing the Real of a senseless bloodbath or sexual violence – in both cases it is, rather, this violence itself which already serves as a fantasized protective shield. Therein lies one of the fundamental lessons of psychoanalysis: the images of utter catastrophe, far from giving access to the Real, can function as a protective shield *against* the Real. In sex as well as in politics, we take refuge in catastrophic scenarios in order to avoid the actual deadlock. In short, the true horror is not the rapist *Urvater* against whom the benevolent maternal father protects us with his fantasy shield, but the benign maternal father himself – the truly suffocating and psychosis-generating experience for the child would have been to have a father like Benigni, who, with his protective care, erases all traces of excessive surplus-enjoyment. It is as a desperate defence measure against *this* father that one fantasizes about the rapist father.

And what if *this* is also the ultimate lesson of Schelling: that the horror of the ultimate *Grund*, this monstrous apparition with hundreds of hands, this vortex that threatens to swallow everything, is a lure, a defence against the abyss of the pure *act*? Another way to approach this same ambiguity and tension in the relationship between fantasy and the Real would be via Heidegger's theme of errancy/untruth as the innermost feature of the event of truth itself. The very opening paragraph of John Sallis's remarkable essay on the monstrosity of truth tackles this difficult point directly:

> What if truth were monstrous? What if it were monstrosity itself, the very condition, the very form, of everything monstrous, everything deformed? But, first of all, itself essentially deformed, monstrous in its very essence? What if there were within the very essence of truth something essentially other than truth, a divergence from nature within nature, true monstrosity?[52]

Before jumping to hasty pseudo-Nietzschean conclusions, let us ponder briefly on what these statements are getting at. Sallis's point is not the pseudo-Nietzschean 'deconstructionist' notion that 'truth' is a fixed, constraining order imposed by some Power on to the free thriving of our life-sustaining imagination – that the 'monstrosity' of truth resides in the fact that every 'regime of truth' deforms and stifles the free flow of our life-energy. For Sallis, as a Heideggerian, Nietzsche, with his famous notion of truth as '*the kind of error* without which a certain kind of living being could not live',[53] remains within the metaphysical opposition between truth and its other (fiction, error, lie), merely accomplishing the anti-Platonic inversion of the relationship between truth and illusion, praising the life-enhancing potential of fictions. Sallis, rather, follows to the end Heidegger's move from truth as *adequatio* to truth as disclosedness: prior to truth as *adequatio* (either *adequatio* of our statements to 'the way things really are' – 'There is a screen in front of me' is true only if there actually is a screen in front of me – or *adequatio* of the things themselves to their essence – 'This is a true hero' if he or she in fact acts as befits the notion of the hero), the thing itself must be disclosed to us as what it is. 'Truth' is thus, for Heidegger, the (historically determined) 'clearing', where things appear to us within a certain horizon of meaning – that is, as part of a certain epochal 'world'. Truth is neither 'subjective' nor 'objective': it designates simultaneously our active engagement *in* and our ex-static openness *to* the world, letting things come forth in their essence. Furthermore, truth as the epochally determined mode of the disclosure of being is not grounded in any transcendental ultimate Foundation (divine Will, evolutionary laws of the universe . . .) – it is in its innermost being an 'event', something that epochally occurs, takes place, 'just happens'. The question is now: how does *this* notion of truth involve an untruth (conceal- ment, errancy, mystery) at its very heart, as its 'essential counter-essence' or 'its proper non-essence'? How are we to think this untruth without reducing it to one of the metaphysical *modi* of the untruth *qua* negative/privative version of truth (lie, illusion, fiction . . .) and, as such, already dependent on truth? When Heidegger speaks of the untruth as inherent to the truth- event itself, he has two different levels in mind:

- On the one hand, the way man, when he is engaged in inner- worldly affairs, forgets the horizon of meaning within which he dwells, and even forgets this forgetting itself (exemplary here is the 'regression' of Greek thought that occurs with the rise of the Sophists: what was a confrontation with the very foundation of our Being turns into a trifling play with differ- ent lines of argumentation, with no inherent relation to truth).
- On the other hand, the way this horizon of meaning itself, in so far as it is an epochal Event, arises against the background of – and thereby conceals – the imponderable Mystery of its emergence, just as a clearing in the midst of a forest is sur- rounded by the dark thickness of the woods.

Leaving aside the difficult question of how these two levels are co-dependent, let us focus on the second, more fundamental level: is it enough to perceive the Untruth in the heart of Truth as the imponderable background against which every epochal truth-event occurs? It seems that even the parallel with Lacan (in so far as we admit it as legitimate) would justify this conclusion: for Lacan also, in order to lie properly, our speech has already in advance to refer to the big Other *qua* the guarantee of Truth – this is why, in contrast to a simple animal feigning, man can *feign to feign*, he can *lie in the guise of truth itself*, like the Jew from the famous anecdote quoted by Freud ('Why are you telling me you're going to Lemberg, when you are really going to Lemberg?').[54] So, for Lacan, the 'untruth' which is *not* in this sense derivative of the dimension of truth would be simply the imponderable thickness of the pre-symbolic Real itself as the unsurpassable background of every symbolic universe. . . . It was William Richardson who – from his unique knowledge of Heidegger *and* Lacan, and in a direct response to Sallis's essay – drew this conclusion when he said: 'When I hear Heidegger talk about *lethe* as "older" than the essence of truth, I hear what Lacan means by the real.'[55]

Here, however, one has to venture a further step, the step whose necessity is indicated by Heidegger himself when, in the elaboration of this notion of an untruth older than the very dimension of truth, he emphasizes how man's 'stepping into the essential unfolding of truth' is a 'transformation of the being of man in the sense of a *derangement* [*Ver-rückung*] of his position among beings'.[56] The 'derangement' to which Heidegger refers is not, of course, a psychological or clinical category: it indicates a much more radical, properly *ontological* reversal/aberration, when the universe itself, in its very foundation, is in a way 'out of joint', thrown off its rails.[57] What is crucial here is to remember that Heidegger wrote these lines in the years of his intensive reading of Schelling's *Treatise on Human Freedom*, a text which discerns the origin of Evil precisely in a kind of *ontological madness*, in the 'derangement' of man's position among beings (his self-centredness); in his early writings, Hegel also refers to such an ontological madness (the 'night of the world', the radical withdrawal of the subject from the world, its radical self-contraction) as a *sine qua non*, a necessary intermediate step ('vanishing mediator') in the passage from 'prehuman nature' to our symbolic universe.[58]

8   Of Stones, Lizards and Men

Does psychoanalysis, perhaps, enable us to delineate further the contours of this ontological madness as the traumatic, properly monstrous ex-timate kernel of truth, other and older than truth, and as such its necessary concealed/withdrawn background/foundation? My contention is that the Freudian death drive, which has nothing whatsoever to do with some 'instinct' that pushes us towards (self-)destruction, is precisely his name for this 'transformation of the being of man in the sense of a *derangement* of his position among beings', for this mysterious/monstrous in-between which is no longer the Real of prehuman nature, of the worldless enclosure of natural entities, and not yet the horizon of Clearing and what comes forth within it, articulated in speech as the 'house of Being', as Heidegger put it in his *Letter on Humanism*, but, rather, the 'deranged'/twisted withdrawn foundation of the horizon of Clearing itself.[59]

And one is tempted to take even a step further along these lines, taking the word 'derangement' quite literally: what, from the psychoanalytic perspective, is the very basic form of human 'derangement'? Is it not the so-called 'fundamental fantasy', this *proton pseudos*, 'primordial lie', older than truth itself, this absolutely idiosyncratic pathological scenario which sustains our being-in-the-world, our dwelling within the symbolic universe, and which, in order to be operative, *has* to remain 'primordially repressed' – that is, to quote Heidegger, the *lethe* (concealment/withdrawal) in the very heart of *aletheia*, of the truth as disclosure. The ontological paradox – scandal, even – of the notion of *fantasy* lies in the fact that it subverts the standard opposition of 'subjective' and 'objective': of course, fantasy is by definition not 'objective' (in the naïve sense of 'existing independently of the subject's perceptions'); however, it is not 'subjective' either (in the sense of being reducible to the subject's consciously experienced intuitions). Fantasy, rather, belongs to the 'bizarre category of the objectively subjective – the way things actually, objectively seem to you even if they don't seem that way to you'.[60]

When, for example, we claim that someone who is consciously well disposed towards Jews none the less harbours profound anti-Semitic prejudices of which he is not consciously aware, do we not claim that (in so far as these prejudices have nothing to do with the way Jews really are, only the way they appear to him) *he is not aware how Jews really seem to him*? Apropos of commodity fetishism, Marx himself uses the term 'objectively necessary appearance'. So, when a critical Marxist encounters a bourgeois subject immersed in commodity fetishism, the Marxist's reproach to him is not 'A commodity may seem to you a magical object endowed with special powers, but really it is just a reified expression of relations between people'; the Marxist's actual reproach is, rather, 'You may think that the commodity appears to you as a simple embodiment of social relations (that, for example, money is just a kind of voucher entitling you to a part of the social product), but *this is not how things really seem to you* – in your social reality, by means of your participation in social exchange, you bear witness to the uncanny fact that a commodity really appears to you as a magical object endowed with special powers'. . . .

This is also one way of specifying the meaning of Lacan's assertion of the subject's constitutive 'decentrement': its point is not that my subjective experience is regulated by objective unconscious mechanisms that are 'decentred' with regard to my self-experience and, as such, beyond my control (a point asserted by every materialist); but, rather, something much more unsettling – I am deprived of even my most intimate 'subjective' experience, the way things 'really seem to me', that of the fundamental fantasy which constitutes and guarantees the core of my being, since I can never consciously experience and assume it. . . . According to the standard view, the dimension which is constitutive of subjectivity is that of phenomenal (self-)experience – I am a subject the moment I can say to myself: 'No matter what unknown mechanism governs my acts, perceptions and thoughts, nobody can take from me what I see and feel now.' Say, when I am passionately in love, and a biochemist informs me that all my intense sentiments are merely the result of biochemical processes in my body, I can answer him by clinging to the appearance: 'All that you're saying may be true; nevertheless, nothing can take from me the intensity of the passion I am experiencing now . . .'.

Lacan's point, however, is that the psychoanalyst is the one who, precisely, *can* take this from the subject – that is to say, his ultimate aim is to deprive the subject of the very fundamental fantasy that regulates the universe of his (self-)experience. The Freudian 'subject of the Unconscious' emerges only when a key aspect of the subject's *phenomenal* (self-)experience (his 'fundamental fantasy') becomes *inaccessible* to him – is 'primordially repressed'. At its most radical, the Unconscious is the *inaccessible phenomenon*, not the objective mechanism that regulates my phenomenal experience. So – in contrast to the commonplace that we are dealing with a subject the moment an entity displays signs of 'inner life', of a fantasmatic self-experience that cannot be reduced to external behaviour – one should claim that what characterizes human subjectivity proper is, rather, the gap that separates the two: the fact that fantasy, at its most elementary, becomes inaccessible to the subject; it is this inaccessibility that makes the subject 'empty'. We thus obtain a relationship that totally subverts the standard notion of the subject who directly experiences himself, his 'inner states': an 'impossible' relationship between the *empty, non-phenomenal subject* and the *phenomena that remain inaccessible to the subject.*[61]

The ultimate *lethe* is thus not the vertiginous abyss of entities beneath the Clearing in which they appear, but the *phenomenon* itself at its most radical, that is, the schema which determines how things appear to us. This scenario literally 'deranges', throws out of joint, the 'proper order of things': it distorts our approach to the world by violently imposing upon it a certain partial perspective. Therein lies the ultimate scandal: when we are dealing with an individual's symptom at its strongest, the entire consistency of a person's self-experience is, in an unacknowledged way, held together by this 'symptomal torsion', by some idiosyncratic pathological tic, so that when we untie this knot (when we disturb a particular, seemingly trifling, point that shouldn't be touched; when we make a trivial remark that shouldn't be uttered . . .), the person's universe literally falls apart. Now let us imagine, in the guise of Schelling's 'naïve' psycho-cosmic speculations, a kind of ontological hyperbole to this matrix, in which a certain 'pathological' singular spin, inaccessible to us 'as such', none the less colours our entire approach to Being, the way entities are disclosed to us. Is not *this* the ultimate *monstrosity* of the truth – that it relies on a pre-ontological obscene idiosyncratic scenario, so that if this scenario is no longer operative, truth itself disintegrates? The paradox is thus that, far from simply deranging/distorting the 'proper balance of things', fantasy at the same time *grounds* every notion of the balanced Universe: fantasy is not an idiosyncratic excess that deranges cosmic order, but the violent singular excess that *sustains* every notion of such an order. Perhaps this is how one can understand Heidegger's notion that metaphysics is unable fully to endorse this interplay of truth and the monstrous concealed kernel at its very heart: the 'illusion' of metaphysics is that this monstrous foreign body is ultimately accidental, affecting not the truth itself but only our access to it – that is, metaphysics is not ready to admit that our distortion of truth is grounded in an inherent distortion constitutive of the truth itself.

How does this gap of monstrosity that underlies truth itself concern the innermost condition of man? In Part Two of *The Fundamental Concepts of Metaphysics*, his course of lectures from 1929 to 1930, Heidegger gets involved in a detailed discussion of the different ontological status of inert objects (stone), animals (lizards, bees) and humans. His famous definition is that the stone is worldless, the animal is poor in world, and man is world-forming, that is, relating to world as such. Leaving aside the specifics of these distinctions – and, more generally, the extraordinary nature of these pages with regard to Heidegger's work (here, Heidegger engages in detailed descriptions of animal behavioural experiments in order to prove his point: he describes how a bee, when its abdomen is cut off, continues to suck the nectar from the flowers, since it has no proper experience of what it means to be satiated . . .) – one should focus on the problematic nature of defining animals as 'poor' with regard to the world: in contrast to a stone, a lizard does somehow relate to stones, sun and so on, around it, but not as humans do.

The problem (of which Heidegger is well aware) is that the designation 'poor' involves an implicit comparison with humans: is it not that an animal appears 'poor' with regard to the world only if we already presuppose the presence of humans as forming their world? In short, is it not that this determination does not define an animal inherently, as it is 'in itself', but already from an anthropomorphic perspective, presupposing humans as the 'measure of all things'? While he acknowledges the problematic and undecided nature of his rumination, Heidegger, towards the end of the chapter concerned with these notions, proposes – in a Schellingian mood – a daring speculative hypothesis that perhaps animals *are*, in a hitherto unknown way, aware of their lack, of the 'poorness' of their relating to the world – perhaps there is an infinite *pain* pervading the whole of living nature: 'if deprivation in certain forms is a kind of suffering, and poverty and deprivation of world belongs to the animal's being, then a kind of pain and suffering would have to permeate the whole animal realm and the realm of life in general'.[62] I said 'in a Schellingian mood', because Schelling wrote about the 'infinite melancholy' of all living nature, about how there is an infinite pain and craving in nature, since nature is caught in an unresolved absolute tension, torn from within, unable to 'reach' or define itself – which is why the emergence of *logos*, of the spoken word, in man is not simply an excess that disturbs the balanced natural circuit but an answer to this infinite pain and deadlock of living nature, a resolution of its unbearable tension; it is as if living nature itself was secretly pointing towards, waiting and longing for, the emergence of *logos* as its redemption.

Before we dismiss this notion as a crazy teleological speculation that belongs to the deservedly forgotten realm of Romantic *Naturphilosophie*, we should nevertheless take a closer look at it. Do we not encounter something similar in historical experience? Let us recall Fellini's *Satyricon*, with its unique depiction of Ancient Roman hedonistic figures permeated by an infinite sadness. Fellini himself claimed that, precisely as a Christian, he wanted to make a film about a universe in which Christianity is yet to come, from which the notion of Christian redemption is totally absent. Does the strange sadness, a kind of fundamental melancholy, of these pagan figures not, then, bear witness to the fact that they somehow already have the premonition that the true God will soon reveal Himself, and that they were born just a little bit too early, so that they cannot be redeemed? And is this not also the fundamental lesson of the Hegelian dialectics of alienation: we are not dealing with the Paradise which is then lost due to some fatal intrusion – there is already in paradisiacal satisfaction (in the satisfaction of the 'naïve' organic community) something suffocating, a longing for fresh air, for an opening that would break the unbearable constraint; and this longing introduces into Paradise an unbearable infinite Pain, a desire to break out – life in Paradise is always pervaded by an infinite melancholy. Perhaps this paradox also accounts for the ultimate paradox of melancholy: melancholy is not primarily directed at the paradisiacal past of organic balanced Wholeness which was lost due to some catastrophe, it is not a sadness caused by this loss; melancholy proper, rather, designates the attitude of those who *are* still in Paradise but are already longing to break out of it: of those who, although still in a closed universe, already possess a vague premonition of another dimension which is just out of their reach, since they came a little bit too early. . . .

Far from entangling us in speculative teleological nonsense, such a reading offers the only way of avoiding the naïve evolutionist approach which sees historical development as the gradual disintegration of primordial organic forms of life (from *Gemeinschaft* to *Gesellschaft*, etc.). On the contrary, it is the evolutionist notion of progress which is inherently teleological, since it conceives of the higher stages as the result of the deployment of the inner potential of the lower stages. In contrast to such an evolutionist notion of progress, one should stick to the notion that the New emerges in order to resolve an unbearable tension in the Old, and was as such already 'present' in the Old in a negative mode, in the guise of an infinite sadness and longing.

This is what, on a totally different level, Walter Benjamin was trying to articulate in his explicitly anti-evolutionist notion of the Messianic promise of a revolutionary Act that will retroactively redeem the Past itself: the present revolution will retroactively realize the crushed longings of all the past, failed revolutionary attempts. What this means is that, in a properly *historical* perspective as opposed to evolutionist historicism, the past is not simply past, but bears within it its proper utopian promise of a future Redemption: in order to understand a past epoch properly, it is not sufficient to take into account the historical conditions out of which it grew – one has also to take into account the utopian hopes of a Future that were betrayed and crushed by it – that which was 'negated', that which did not happen – so that the past historical reality was the way it was. To conceive the French Revolution, one has to focus also on the utopian hopes of liberation that were crushed by its final outcome, the common bourgeois reality – and the same goes for the October Revolution. Thus we are dealing not with idealist or spiritualist teleology, but with the dialectical notion of a historical epoch whose 'concrete' definition has to include its crushed potentials, which were inherently 'negated' by its reality.

To put it in even clearer terms: when we say that the present redeems the past itself, that the past itself contained signs which pointed towards the present, we are not making a historicist-relativist statement about how there is no 'objective' history; how we always interpret the past from our present horizon of understanding; how, in defining past epochs, we always – consciously or not – imply our present point of view. What we are claiming is something much more radical: what the proper *historical* stance (as opposed to historicism) 'relativizes' is not the past (always distorted by our present point of view) but, paradoxically, *the present itself* – our present can be conceived only as the outcome (not of what actually happened in the past, but also) of the crushed potentials for the future that were contained in the past. In other words, it is not only – as Foucault liked to emphasize, in a Nietzschean mode – that every history of the past is ultimately the 'ontology of the present', that we always perceive our past within the horizon of our present preoccupations, that in dealing with the past we are in effect dealing with the ghosts of the past whose resuscitation enables us to confront our present dilemmas. It is also that we, the 'actual' present historical agents, have to conceive of *ourselves* as the materialization of the ghosts of past generations, as the stage in which these past generations retro-actively resolve their deadlocks.

How, then, are we to answer the automatic criticism that such a melancholic presentiment of the future can be perceived only if we read the past from the perspective of the future – that is, dis-torted through teleological lenses? Is it not that this melancholic presentiment was not 'really there', but is just a kind of perspec-tive distortion, read into the past from our later standpoint? (This situation is not unlike the well-known circular explanation of the emergence of language, one of the elementary matrixes of ideology: 'people invented language signs because they had something to say to each other' – as if, before language, there was already a need for it . . .) However, did not Marx show us the way out of this predicament when he emphasized that it is man who provides the key to the anatomy of the ape, not vice versa? In other words, the mistake of the evolutionist perspective is to accept the 'obvious' presupposition that the past was simply there, fully ontologically constituted, not 'open', containing the traces that were pointing towards the future.

This problematic also enables us to throw some new light on a certain fundamental oscillation in Lacan: what comes first, the signifier or some deadlock in the Real? Sometimes, Lacan pre-sents the traumatic colonization of the live body by the parasitic symbol Order as the primordial fact: it is the intervention of the Symbolic that derails, throws out of joint, the natural organism in its balanced circuit, transforming natural instincts into a mon-strous drive that can never be fully satisfied, since it is condemned to an eternal 'undead' returning to its path, persisting forever in an obscene immortality. At other times, in a more speculative-mythical mode, he is searching for some kind of natural excess or imbalance, a malfunctioning, monstrous derailment, and then he conceives the symbolic Order as a secondary in(ter)vention destined to 'gentrify' this monstrous excess, to resolve its deadlock. One is tempted to claim that it is here, between these two versions, that the line runs which separates materialism from idealism: the primacy of the symbolic Order is clearly idealist; it is ultimately a new version of Divine intervention in the natural order; while the second version – the emergence of the symbolic Order as the answer to some monstrous excess in the Real – is the only proper materialist solution.

9   The Structure and its Event

This means that the relationship between the Structure and its Event is indeterminable. On the one hand, the Event is the impossible Real of a structure, of its synchronous symbolic order, the engendering violent gesture which brings about the legal Order that renders this very gesture retroactively 'illegal', relegating it to the spectral repressed status of something that can never be fully acknowledged–symbolized–confessed. In short, the synchronous structural Order is a kind of defence-formation against its grounding Event which can be discerned only in the guise of a mythical spectral narrative. On the other hand, one can also claim the exact opposite: is not the status of this Event itself (the mythical narrative of the primordial violent founding gesture) ultimately fantasmatic; is it not a fantasy-construction destined to account for the unaccountable (the origins of the Order) by concealing, rendering invisible, the Real of the structural antagonism (deadlock, impossibility) that prevents the structural synchronous Order from achieving its balance? In short, is not the Event of the primordial crime secondary, a retroactive 'projection' destined to translate/transpose the synchronous antagonism/deadlock into the diachronous narrative succession? The loop is therefore perfect: the Structure can function only through the occultation of the violence of its founding Event, yet the very narrative of this Event is ultimately nothing but a fantasy destined to resolve the debilitating antagonism/inconsistency of the structuring/synchronous Order. So, again, one has to distinguish between the impossible Real of the 'timeless' antagonism and the fantasmatic primordially repressed narrative which serves as the unacknowledged yet necessary spectral supplement.

With regard to the notion of the act as real, this means that an authentic *act* is in between Time and Eternity. On the one hand, an act is, as Kant and Schelling have put it, the point at which 'eternity intervenes in time', at which the enchainment of temporal causal succession is interrupted, at which 'something emerges-intervenes out of nothing', at which something takes place which cannot be explained away as the outcome/result of the preceding chain (to put it in Kant's terms, the act designates the direct intervention of the noumenal dimension into phenomenality; to put it in Schelling's terms, the act designates the moment at which the abyssal/atemporal principle of identity – 'I did it because I did it, for no particular reason' – momentarily suspends the reign of the principle of sufficient reason). On the other hand, the act is at the same time the moment of the emergence of time in/from eternity: as Schelling put it, the act is the primordial decision/separation [*Ent-Scheidung*] that represses into an eternal past the deadlock of pure simultaneity; it 'breaks the deadlock' by disturbing the balance, by 'unilaterally' privileging some aspect of the undifferentiated Whole over all other aspects.[63] In short, an act proper is the paradox of the time-less/'eternal' gesture of overcoming eternity, opening up the dimension of temporality/historicity.

In order to grasp this crucial point, one has to bear in mind that there is no 'time as such', there are only concrete horizons of temporality/historicity, each horizon grounded in a primordial act of foreclosure, of 'repression' of its own founding gesture. To put it in Ernesto Laclau's terms: antagonism is such a point of 'eternity' of the social constellation defined by this antagonism, the point of reference that generates the historical process as the attempt to resolve it.[64] In Judith Butler's terms, the 'passionate attachment' would perhaps be a candidate for such a dialectical 'eternity' – the primordially repressed/disavowed libidinal con-stellation that is not simply historical–temporal, since its very repression generates and sustains the multiple modes of histori-cization.[65]

Even such an apparently trivial domain as fashion provides a nice example of how ideology displaces/conceals class antago-nism: the fashion for stonewashed jeans, for instance, imaginarily resolves class antagonism by offering jeans which can be appropriated by those who are 'down' and those who are 'up' – the upper strata wear stonewashed jeans in order to appear in solidarity with popular strata, while members of the popular strata wear them in order to look like members of the upper strata. So when members of the lower strata wear stonewashed jeans, the seemingly direct coincidence between social status (poverty) and clothing (worn, torn jeans) masks a double medi-ation: they are imitating those who are imitating an imagined popular working-class look. . . . The ultimate irony here is that the company which specializes in such products – destined to blur/displace the class gap – is called, precisely, *Gap*. The important theoretical lesson of Gap for a Marxist is therefore that every assertion of a class position is thoroughly differential/dialogical: not only in the sense that each position asserts itself through the contrast to the opposite position, but also – and even primarily – in the sense that the assertion of position A always-already functions in a minimally reflexive way, as a kind of pre-emptive strike – it answers the possible reproach of B (its opposite) in advance by displacing/blurring the gap that separates it from B. So, with regard to fashion: it is not only that each class or stratum has its own fashion, which 'expresses' its position; it is not only that this fashion is not defined intrinsically, but always in contrast to the fashion of its opposite (French workers wear berets *because their bosses do not wear them*); the point is, rather, that the fashion identified with a certain stratum is always mediated by the fashion of its structural opposite, endeavouring to displace this opposition. Reflexivity is primordial here: there *never was* an originary 'innocent' moment when each stratum wore its 'proper' clothes (the lower strata stonewashed jeans; the upper strata well-pressed black trousers); from the very beginning, the class opposition was displaced, caught in the reflexivity of pre-emptive strikes and displacements.

Now we can also risk the precise formulation of the proper dialectical relationship between eternity and time. 'Eternity' is not atemporal in the simple sense of persisting *beyond* time; it is, rather, the name for the Event or Cut that sustains, opens up, the dimension of temporality as the series/succession of failed attempts to grasp it. The psychoanalytic name for this

Event/Cut is, of course, *trauma*. Trauma is 'eternal'; it can never be properly temporalized/historicized, it is the point of 'eternity' around which time circulates – that is to say, it is an Event accessible within time only through its multiple traces. Eternity and time (in the sense of temporalization/historicization) are thus far from being simply opposed: in a sense, there is no time without eternity: temporality is sustained by our failure to grasp/symbolize/historicize the 'eternal' trauma. If trauma were to be successfully temporalized/historicized, the very dimension of time would implode/collapse into a timeless eternal Now. This is the point to be made against historicism: that it fails to take into account the reference to some traumatic point of Eternity that sustains temporality itself. If, then, we claim that each concrete historical constellation generates its own eternity, this does *not* simply mean that Eternity is the ideological myth generated by historical reality: Eternity is, rather, that which is *excluded* so that historical reality can maintain its consistency.

Of special interest here are the theological consequences of these considerations. Pre-Christian religions remain at the level of 'wisdom'; they emphasize the insufficiency of every temporal finite object, and preach either moderation in pleasures (one should avoid excessive attachment to finite objects, since pleasure is transitory) or the withdrawal from temporal reality in favour of the True Divine Object which alone can provide Infinite Bliss. Christianity, on the contrary, offers Christ as a mortal-temporal individual, and insists that belief in the *temporal* Event of Incarnation is the only path to *eternal* truth and salvation. In this precise sense, Christianity is a 'religion of Love': in love, one singles out, focuses on, a finite temporal object which 'means more than anything else'. This same paradox is also at work in the specific Christian notion of Conversion and the forgiveness of sins: Conversion is a *temporal event* which changes *eternity itself*. The later Kant articulated the notion of the noumenal act of choice by means of which an individual chooses his eternal character and which therefore, prior to his temporal existence, delineates in advance the contours of his terrestrial destiny.[66] Without the Divine act of Grace, our destiny would remain immovable, forever fixed by this eternal act of choice; the 'good news' of Christianity, however, is that, in a genuine Conversion, one can 're-create' oneself, that is, *repeat* this act, and thus *change (undo the effects of) eternity itself*.

Here we approach the crux of the matter, the delicate question of the relationship between Judaism and Christianity. Judaism, with its 'stubborn attachment' (Judith Butler's term again) to the unacknowledged violent founding gesture that haunts the public legal order as its spectral supplement, is not only split within itself between its 'public' aspect of the symbolic Law and its obscene underside (the 'virtual' narrative of the irredeemable excess of violence that established the very rule of Law) – this split is at the same time the split between Judaism and Christianity. The paradox of Judaism is that it maintains fidelity to the founding violent Event precisely by *not* confessing–symbolizing it: this 'repressed' status of the Event is what gives Judaism its unprecedented vitality; it is what enabled the Jews to persist and survive for thousands of years without land or a common institutional tradition. In short, the Jews did not *give up the ghost*; they survived all their ordeals precisely because they refused to *give up their ghost*, to cut off the link to their secret, disavowed tradition. Christianity, on the other hand, is the religion of *confession*: as Freud himself emphasized in *Moses and Monotheism*, the Christians are ready to *confess* the primordial crime (in the displaced form of murdering not the Father but Christ, the son of God), and thereby *betray* its traumatic impact/weight, pretending that it is possible to come to terms with it.

Against this background, one can properly locate Foucault's thesis that psychoanalysis is the last, conclusive term in the confessionary mode of discourse that began with early Christianity:[67] if those who emphasize that psychoanalysis is in its very substance continually marked by a Jewish attitude, and that this 'Jewishness' continued against all attempts to render it Gentile and cut its Jewish umbilical cord (including those of Freud himself, when he designated Jung as his heir), are right, then one must draw the unavoidable conclusion that psychoanalysis, far from being a confessionary mode of discourse, entails the acceptance and admission that all our discursive formations are forever haunted by some 'indivisible remainder', by some traumatic spectral 'rest' that resists 'confession', that is, integration into the symbolic universe – or, in Christian terms, that can never be redeemed–delivered, laid to rest, pacified/gentrified. The Freudian name for this 'undead' remainder is, of course, again *trauma* – it is the implicit reference to some traumatic kernel which persists as the obscene/monstrous 'undead' remainder, which keeps a discursive universe 'alive' – that is to say, there is no life without the supplement of the obscene–undead spectral persistence of the 'living dead'. Consequently, the ultimate goal of psychoanalysis is not the confessionary pacification/gentrification of the trauma, but the acceptance of the very fact that our lives involve a traumatic kernel beyond redemption, that there is a dimension of our being which forever resists redemption–deliverance.

To put it in yet another way: Judaism stands for the paradox of Universalism which maintains its universal dimension precisely by its 'passionate attachment' to the stain of particularity that serves as its unacknowledged foundation. Judaism thus not only belies the common-sense notion that the price to be paid for access to universality is to renounce one's particularity; it also demonstrates how the stain of unacknowledgeable particularity of the gesture that generates the Universal is the ultimate resource of the Universal's vitality: cut off from irredeemable/repressed particular roots, the Universal ossifies and changes into a lifeless, empty, abstract universal form. Or – to put it in even more specific terms – Judaism, as it were, ironically reverses the standard Marxist procedure of discerning in the assertion of some abstract Universal the particular content that actually hegemonizes it ('the universal rights of man are effectively the rights of . . . [white male property owners]'): its implicit claim is that the actual content of Jewish 'particularism', of its stubborn sticking to a set of arbitrary particular prescriptions, is none other than the assertion of actual Universality.

At this precise point, however, things become complicated. Does Christianity really stand for the passage from the universality that continues to maintain the link with the excessive violence of its particular Ground, the source of its vitality, to the universality that obliterates the traces of this contingent violence – that achieves Redemption by coming to terms with its traumatic Origins, by ritualistically enacting the founding Crime and the Sacrifice that erases its traces, by bringing about reconciliation in the medium of the Word? What if the split between the symbolic Law and the obscene shadowy supplement of excessive violence that sustains it is *not* the ultimate horizon of our experience? What if this entanglement of Law and its spectral double is precisely what, in the famous passage from Romans 7: 7, Saint Paul denounces as that which the intervention of the Christian *agape* (love as charity) enables us to leave behind? What if the Pauline *agape*, the move beyond the mutual implication of Law and sin, is *not* the step towards the full symbolic integration of the particularity of Sin into the universal domain of the Law, but its exact opposite, the unheard-of gesture of leaving behind the domain of the Law itself, of 'dying to the Law', as Saint Paul put it (Romans 7:5)? In other words, what if the Christian wager is *not* Redemption in the sense of the possibility for the domain of the universal Law retroactively to 'sublate' – integrate, pacify, erase – its traumatic origins, but something radically different, the cut into the Gordian knot of the vicious cycle of Law and its founding Transgression?

What many people may find problematic in the Pauline *agape* is that it seems to *superegotize* love, conceiving it in an almost Kantian way – not as a spontaneous overflow of generosity, not as a self-assertive stance, but as a self-suppressing *duty* to love neighbours and care for them, as hard *work*, as something to be accomplished through the strenuous effort of fighting and inhibiting one's spontaneous 'pathological' inclinations. As such, *agape* is opposed to *eros*, which designates not so much carnal lust as, rather, the kindness and care that are part of one's nature, and whose accomplishment delivers its own satisfaction. But is this, in fact, Saint Paul's position? Would this stance attributed to Saint Paul not be, rather, love *within the confines of the Law*, love as the struggle to suppress the excess of sin generated by the Law? And is not the true *agape* closer to the modest dispensing of spontaneous goodness?[68]

In the final scene of Kieslowski's film *Blue*, this Pauline *agape* is given its ultimate cinematic expression. While Julie, the heroine, sits in bed after making love, in one continuous long shot (accompanied by the choral rendition of the lines on love from I Corinthians), the camera covers four different scenes, slowly drifting from one to the other; these scenes present the persons to whom Julie is intimately related: Antoine, the boy who witnessed the fatal car crash in which her husband and children died; Julie's mother, sitting silent in her room in an old people's home; Lucille, her young striptease dancer friend, at work on the stage in a nightclub; Sandrine, her dead husband's mistress, touching her naked belly in the last phase of pregnancy, bearing the unborn child of her deceased lover. . . . The continuous drift from one set to another (they are separated only by a dark blurred background across which the camera pans) creates the effect of mysterious synchronicity which somehow recalls the famous 360-degree shot in Hitchcock's *Vertigo*: after Judy is fully transformed into Madeleine, the couple passionately embrace, and while the camera makes a full circle around them, the scene darkens and the background which indicates the setting (Judy's hotel room) changes to the site of Scottie's last embrace with Madeleine (the barn of the San Juan Batista mission) and then again back to the hotel room, as if, in a continuous dreamlike space, the camera passes from one stage to another within an indefinite dreamscape in which individual scenes emerge out of darkness. How, then, are we to read this unique shot from *Blue*? The key is provided by the way this shot is related to another unique shot from the beginning of the film, when, after the crash, Julie is in her hospital bed, lying silent in the atavistic state of complete shock. In an extreme close-up, almost the entire frame is filled by her eye, and we see the objects in the hospital room reflected in this eye as derealized spectral apparitions of partial objects – it seems as if this shot encapsulates Hegel's famous passage about the 'night of the world':

> The human being is this night, this empty nothing, that contains everything in its simplicity – an unending wealth of many representations, images, of which none belongs to him – or which are not present. This night, the interior of nature, that exists here – pure self – in phantasmagorical representations, is night all around it, in which here shoots a bloody head – there another white ghastly apparition, suddenly here before it, and just so disappears. One catches sight of this night when one looks human beings in the eye – into a night that becomes awful.[69]

The parallel with *Vertigo* imposes itself again here: in the (deservedly) famous credits sequence, strange graphic shapes which seem to announce the 'strange attractors' of chaos theory (developed decades after the film was shot) emerge out of the darkness of a woman's eye. The close-up of the eye from *Blue* stands for the symbolic death of Julie: not her real (biological) death, but the suspension of the links with her symbolic environment; while the final shot stands for the reassertion of life. The interconnection of the two shots is thus clear: they both represent a scene which is fantasmatic – in both cases, we see partial objects floating in a dark background of the Void (of the eye in the first case; of the unspecified darkness of the screen in the second). The tonality, however, is different: from the reduction of all reality into the spectral reflection in the eye, we pass to the ethereal lightness of scenes whose reality (of being part of particular life-situations) is also suspended, but in the direction of a pure synchronicity, of an almost mystical standstill, of a time-less Now in which different scenes, torn out of their particular contexts, vibrate in each other. The two shots thus stage the two opposed aspects of *freedom*: the 'abstract' freedom of pure self-relating negativity, withdrawal-into-self, cutting of the links with reality; and the 'concrete' freedom of the loving acceptance of others, of experiencing oneself as free, as finding full realization in relating to others. To put it in Schelling's terms, the passage from the first to the second is the passage from extreme egotistic *contraction* to boundless *expansion*. So when, at the end of this scene, Julie cries (which, until this moment, she has not been able to do), her work of mourning is accomplished, she is recon-ciled with the universe; her tears are not the tears of sadness and pain, but the tears of *agape*, of a Yes! to life in its mysterious synchronic multitude.[70]

Another way to approach this same problem would be through the theme of iconoclasm. The usual argument is that pagan (pre-Jewish) gods were 'anthropomorphic' (Ancient Greek gods fornicated, cheated, and engaged in other ordinary human pas-sions . . .), while the Jewish religion, with its iconoclasm, was the first thoroughly to 'de-anthropomorphize' Divinity. What, how-ever, if things are the exact opposite? What if the very need to prohibit man from making images of God bears witness to the 'personification' of God discernible in God's saying 'Let us make humankind in our image, according to our likeness' (Genesis 1: 26) – what if the true target of Jewish iconoclastic prohibition were not previous pagan religions but, rather, *its own* 'anthropo-morphization'/'personalization' of God? What if the Jewish religion *itself* generates the very excess it has to prohibit? In pagan religions, such prohibition would have been *meaningless*. (And Christianity then goes a step further by asserting not only the likeness of God and man, but their direct *identity* in the figure of Christ: 'no wonder man looks like God, since *the* man [Christ] *is* God'.) According to the standard notion, pagans were anthropomorphic, Jews were radically iconoclastic, and Christianity operates a kind of 'synthesis', a partial regression to paganism, by introducing the ultimate 'icon to erase all other icons', that of the suffering Christ. Against this argument, one should assert that it is the Jewish religion which remains an 'abstract/immediate' negation of anthropomorphism, and as such attached to it, determined by it in its very direct negation, whereas it is only Christianity that actually 'sublates' paganism.

On the imaginary level, man is made directly in the image/likeness of God. The Jewish religion is an immediate negation of this: You must not depict God; God has no face accessible to us. Christianity, on the other hand, no longer needs this prohibition, because it knows that face–image is an *appearance*. In a sentimental answer to a child asking what God's face looks like, a priest replied that whenever the child encounters a human face radiating benevolence and goodness, whomsoever this face belongs to, he catches a glimpse of His face. The truth of this sentimental platitude is that the Suprasensible (God's face) is discernible as a momentary, fleeting appearance, a 'grimace', of an earthly face. It is in *this* sense (an 'appearance' which, as it were, transubstantiates a piece of reality into something that, for a brief moment, radiates the suprasensible Eternity) that man is like God: in both cases, the structure is that of an *appearance*, of a sublime dimension that *appears through* the sensible image of the face – or, as Lacan puts it, following Hegel, the suprasensible is the appearance as such . . . Butler's critical point that the Lacanian Symbolic is merely a *hegemonic imaginary*[71] can therefore be accepted – on condition that one defines 'hegemony' in the strict Laclauian way, not merely as the elevation of a certain imaginary matrix into a global reified/codified rule and/or model. That is to say: the difference between Imaginary proper and Symbolic *qua* Imaginary 'as such' is that of the competition between Zeuxis and Parrhasios from the Ancient Greek anecdote often cited by Lacan: one was duped by the image itself, taking the painted birds for the 'real' ones; while the other, confronted with the painted veil, told the painter: 'OK, take the veil away, uncover the painting behind it!' In this second case, the image deceives us not by seducing us into taking the painted object for the 'real thing', but by making us believe that there is a 'real thing' concealed beneath it – and, in this second case, the deception of the image is properly symbolic. The symbolic dimension proper is thus that of *appearance* – appearance as, precisely, opposed to imaginary simulacrum. In a sublime appearance, the positive imaginary content is a stand-in for the 'impossible' Beyond (the Thing, God, Freedom . . .) – just as, for Laclau, 'hegemony means the representation, by a particular [content], of an impossible totality with which it is incommensurable'.[72] In short, the moment we enter the dimension of symbolic appearance, the imaginary content is caught/inscribed in a dialectic of void and negativity.[73]

In philosophy, it was Schelling who revealed how the Christian 'humanization' of God in no way involves the anthropomorphic reduction of God to a human phantasmic creation. Schelling's direct anthropological texts tend to be rather boring and disappointing; however, when he evokes anthropological themes (or, rather, insights into the human psyche) as 'illustrations' or metaphors to explain his most abstract theosophical ruminations (say, when, in order to explain the Divine pronouncement of the Word which resolves the deadlock of God's debilitating madness, he evokes the common psychological experience of how the act of suddenly 'finding the right word' resolves the preceding protracted and incapacitating indecision), the result is eye-opening in a truly breathtaking way. This discrepancy should warn us against the common reductionist claim that Schelling's mythopoeic narrative of what went on in God's mind before the creation of the world is simply a mystified presentation of deep psychological observations – such a reductive reading of Schelling as a coded depth psychologist somehow misses the point.

Here one is tempted to repeat Adorno's well-known reversal of Croce's patronizing historicist question about 'what is dead and what is alive in Hegel's dialectic' (the title of his most important work):[74] the question to be raised today is not the historicist one of 'How does Schelling's work stand with regard to today's constellation? How are we to read it, so that it will still say something to us?', but 'How do we today *stand with regard to – in the eyes of – Schelling?*'. Furthermore, the same reversal must be applied to the very relationship between God and man: Schelling's problem is not 'What does God mean in our – human – eyes? Does He still mean anything? Is it possible to account for human history without any reference to God? Is God just a projection of human fantasies?', but the *opposite* one: '*What does* man *mean in the eyes of God?*' That is to say: one should never forget that Schelling's starting point is always God, the Absolute itself; consequently, his problem is: 'What role does the emergence of man play in the Divine life? Why – in order to

resolve what kind of deadlock – did God have to create man?'
Within this context, the criticism of 'anthropomorphism' apropos
of Schelling's use of psychological observations in his description
of the Divine life again misses the point: 'anthropomorphism' in
the description of the Divine life is not only not to be avoided; it
is, rather, to be openly endorsed – not because man is 'similar' to
God, but because man directly *is* part of the Divine life, that is,
because it is only in man, in human history, that God fully real-
izes Himself, that He becomes an actual living God.

10   From the Decalogue to Human Rights

Against today's onslaught of New Age neo-paganism, it thus
seems both theoretically productive and politically salient to stick
to Judaeo-Christian logic. Along these neo-pagan lines, John
Gray, author of *Men are from Mars, Women are from Venus*, recently
proposed, in a series of Oprah Winfrey shows, a vulgarized
version of narrativist-deconstructionist psychoanalysis: since we
ultimately 'are' the stories we are telling ourselves about ourselves, the solution to a psychic deadlock lies in a 'positive'
creative rewriting of the narrative of our past. What Gray has in
mind is not only the standard cognitive therapy of changing negative 'false beliefs' about oneself into a more positive attitude of
the assurance that one is loved by others and capable of creative
achievements, but a more 'radical', pseudo-Freudian notion of
regressing back to the scene of the primordial traumatic wound.
That is to say: Gray accepts the psychoanalytic notion of a hard
kernel of some early childhood traumatic experience that forever

marked the subject's further development, giving it a pathological turn – what he proposes is that after regressing to his primal traumatic scene, and thus directly confronting it, the subject should, under the therapist's guidance, 'rewrite' this scene, this ultimate phantasmic framework of his subjectivity, as a more 'positive', benign and productive narrative – if, say, your primordial traumatic scene that persisted in your unconscious, distorting and inhibiting your creative attitude, was that of your father shouting at you: 'You're worthless! I despise you! Nothing good will come out of you!', you should rewrite it into a new scene with a benevolent father smiling kindly at you and telling you: 'You're OK! I trust you completely!' (In one of these Oprah Winfrey shows, Gray directly enacted this rewriting-the-past experience with a woman who, at the end, gratefully embraced him, crying with happiness that she was no longer haunted by her father's contemptuous attitude towards her.) To play this game to the end: when the Wolf Man 'regressed' to the traumatic scene that determined his subsequent psychic development – witnessing the parental *coitus a tergo* – the solution would be to rewrite this scene, so that what the Wolf Man actually saw was merely his parents lying on the bed, Father reading a newspaper and Mother a sentimental novel.

Ridiculous as this procedure may appear, let us not forget that it also has its PC version – that of ethnic, sexual, etc., minorities rewriting their past in a more positive, self-assertive vein (African-Americans claiming that long before European modernity, Ancient African empires already had highly developed science and technology, etc.). Along the same lines, one can even imagine a rewriting of the Decalogue itself: is some commandment too severe? Let us regress to the scene on Mount

Sinai and rewrite it: adultery – yes, if it is sincere, and serves the goal of your profound self-realization. . . . What disappears in this total reduction of the past to its subsequent retroactive rewriting is not primarily the 'hard facts' but the Real of a traumatic encounter whose structuring role in the subject's psychic economy forever resists its symbolic rewriting.

This mention of the Decalogue was far from accidental: in our Western tradition, the exemplary case of such a traumatic Real is the Jewish Law. Let us not forget that, in the Jewish tradition, the Divine Mosaic Law is experienced as *externally imposed, contingent and traumatic* – in short, as an impossible/real Thing that 'makes the law'. What is arguably the ultimate scene of religious-ideological interpellation – the pronouncement of the Decalogue on Mount Sinai – is the very opposite of something that emerges 'organically' as the outcome of the path of self-knowing and self-realization. The Judaeo-Christian tradition is thus to be strictly opposed to the New Age Gnostic problematic of self-realization or self-fulfilment: when the Old Testament enjoins you to love and respect your neighbour, this refers not to your imaginary *semblable*/double, but to the neighbour *qua* traumatic Thing. In contrast to the New Age attitude which ultimately reduces my Other/Neighbour to my mirror-image, or to a step along the path of my own self-realization (like Jungian psychology, in which others around me are ultimately reduced to externalizations/projections of the different disavowed aspects of my own personality), Judaism opens up a tradition in which an alien traumatic kernel forever persists in my Neighbour – the Neighbour remains an inert, impenetrable, enigmatic presence that *hystericizes* me. (Another aspect of this same constellation – the reverse of the fact that the Jewish God is emptied of *jouissance*, reduced to a self-referential Name, to the subjectivity of a pure, non-substantial enunciator – is that the only terrain on which to demonstrate your devotion to the Divine Law is that of 'love for thy neighbour', of your social-ethical activity – again, there is no direct short cut to contact with the Divine dimension through the 'inner path' of mystical spiritual self-realization.) Against this background, one can also see in what precise sense Lacan is radically *anti-narrativist*: in his insistence on how the encounter with the symbolic Law is the encounter with some traumatic, impenetrable Real, Lacan directly inscribes psychoanalysis into the Judaic tradition.

It is also crucial to bear in mind the interconnection between the Decalogue (the traumatically imposed Divine Commandments) and its modern obverse, the celebrated 'human Rights'.[75] As the experience of our post-political liberal-permissive society amply demonstrates, human Rights are ultimately, at their core, simply *Rights to violate the Ten Commandments*. 'The right to privacy' – the right to *adultery*, in secret, where no one sees me or has the right to probe into my life. 'The right to pursue happiness and to possess private property' – the right to *steal* (to exploit others). 'Freedom of the press and of the expression of opinion' – the right to *lie*. 'The right of free citizens to possess weapons' – the right to *kill*. And, ultimately, 'freedom of religious belief' – the right to worship false gods. Of course, human Rights do not *directly* condone the violation of the Ten Commandments – the point is simply that they keep open a marginal 'grey zone' which should remain out of reach of (religious or secular) power: in this shady zone, I can violate these commandments, and if power probes into it, catching me with my pants down and trying to prevent my violations, I can cry: 'Assault on my basic human

Rights!'. The point is thus that it is structurally impossible, for Power, to draw a clear line of separation and prevent only the 'misuse' of a Right, while not encroaching upon the proper use, that is, the use that does *not* violate the Commandments.[76]

There is a somewhat analogous situation with regard to the heterosexual seduction procedure in our Politically Correct times: the two sets, the set of PC behaviour and the set of seduction, do not actually intersect anywhere; that is, there is no seduction which is not in a way an 'incorrect' intrusion or harassment – at some point, one has to expose oneself and 'make a pass'. So does this mean that every seduction is incorrect harassment through and through? No, and that is the catch: when you make a pass, you expose yourself to the Other (the potential partner), and she decides retroactively, by her reaction, whether what you have just done was harassment or a successful act of seduction – and there is no way to tell in advance what her reaction will be. This is why assertive women often despise 'weak' men – because they fear to expose themselves, to take the necessary risk. And perhaps this is even more true in our PC times: are not PC prohibitions rules which, in one way or another, are to be violated in the seduction process? Is not the seducer's art to accomplish this violation properly – so that afterwards, by its acceptance, its harassing aspect will be retroactively cancelled?

Is not the opposition between the commandments of the Decalogue and human Rights grounded already in the tension between the Decalogue and the injunction to 'love thy neighbour'? This injunction prohibits nothing; rather, it calls for an activity *beyond* the confines of the Law, enjoining us always to do more and more, to 'love' our neighbour – not merely in his imaginary dimension (as our *semblant*, mirror-image, on behalf of the notion of Good that we impose on him, so that even when we act and help him 'for his own Good', it is *our* notion of what is good for him that we follow); not merely in his symbolic dimension (the abstract symbolic subject of Rights), but as the Other in the very abyss of its Real, the Other as a properly *inhuman* partner, 'irrational', radically evil, capricious, revolting, disgusting . . . in short, beyond the Good. This enemy–Other should not be punished (as the Decalogue demands), but accepted as a 'neighbour'.[77] (Tim Robbins's outstanding film *Dead Man Walking* stages this very deadlock of the 'love for one's neighbour': Sister Helen goes to the end, accepting the humanity of the Other, who is the most worthless racist and murderous rapist scum.) There is a double defence against this thorough 'love of thy neighbour': rationalist/humanist 'understanding' (we try to reduce the Other's traumatic abyss by explaining it as the result of social, ideological, psychological, etc. conditioning . . .), or the fetishization of the radical Evil of our neighbour into the absolute Otherness (say, of the Holocaust) which is thus rendered untouchable, unpoliticizable, impossible to be accounted for in terms of a power struggle.

One can see how human rights and 'love for thy neighbour' *qua* Real are the two aspects of the same gesture of going beyond the Decalogue: the ultimate 'subject of human Rights' is precisely the Neighbour as the real/impossible *Ding* beyond the reach of the Law – the '(human) right' is the infinite right of the abyss of subjectivity beyond the Law. The Jewish refusal to assert love for the neighbour outside the confines of the Law aims at preventing this love from degrading into a narcissistic (mis)recognition of my mirror-image – is it possible, however, to conceive of love for the Other *qua* Thing which simultaneously avoids narcissistic

regression *and* remains outside the confines of the Law? The ultimate answer of the injunction 'love thy neighbour' is *Yes!*:
imaginary mirror relationships *and* the symbolic Law are precisely the two *defences* against the Neighbour *qua* Real. One can
also see, however, how human Rights are not simply opposed to
the Ten Commandments, but are the 'inherent transgression'[78]
generated by those Commandments – there is no space for human
Rights outside the terrain of the Decalogue. Here one should
recall again Saint Paul's famous passage on the interconnection
between Law and sin – on how Law itself generates sinful desires.
As Lacan pointed out, the very text of the Decalogue is ambiguous here: 'You will adore no God *before my countenance*': 'Does it
mean that beyond the countenance of God, i.e., outside Canaan,
the adoration of other gods is not inconceivable for a faithful
Jew?'[79] In other words, does it mean that the important point is
simply to maintain appearances – you can do it in private, where
the big Other cannot see you? Does it mean that the jealous God
of the Decalogue was like a wife whose message to her unfaithful
husband is: 'Do it, just do it so that I won't learn anything about
it!' And what does Christianity do here? Does it simply 'close up
the space' by prohibiting even the inherent transgression: by
demanding that we follow God's commandments not only 'before
His countenance', but also deep in our hearts? Or does it endeavour to break the very vicious cycle of Law/sin?

11   The Principle of Charity

So, again: in what, precisely, does the elementary Christian gesture – best designated by Pauline *agape* – consist? In *Inquiries into*

Truth and Interpretation, Donald Davidson developed what he calls the Principle of Charity, a 'charitable assumption about human intelligence that might turn out to be false':[80] 'disagreement and agreement alike are intelligible only against a background of massive agreement'[81] – that is to say: 'what makes interpretation possible is the fact that we can dismiss a priori the chance of massive error'.[82] As Davidson emphasizes, this assumption is not simply a choice we can make or not make but a kind of a priori of speech, a presupposition we silently adopt and follow the moment we engage in communication with others:

> Since charity is not an option, but a condition of having a workable theory, it is meaningless to suggest that we might fall into massive error by endorsing it. . . . Charity is forced on us; whether we like it or not, if we want to understand others, we must count them right in most matters.[83]

Davidson's Principle of Charity is therefore another name for the Lacanian 'big Other' as the ultimate guarantee of Truth to which we have to make reference even when we are lying or trying to deceive our partners in communication, precisely in order to be successful in our deceit. One should bear in mind, however, that Lacan, in the last decades of his teaching, severely qualified this status of the big Other twice:

- First when, as early as the late 1950s, he emphasized the fact that the 'quilting point', the quasi-transcendental Master-Signifier that guarantees the consistency of the big Other, is ultimately a *fake*, an empty signifier without a signified. Suffice it to recall how a community functions: the Master-Signifier which guarantees the community's consistency is a signifier whose signified is an enigma for the members themselves – nobody really knows what it means, but each of them somehow presupposes that others know, that it has to mean 'the real thing', so they use it all the time. . . . This logic is at work not only in politico-ideological links (with different terms for the *cosa nostra*: our nation, revolution . . .), but even in some Lacanian communities where the group recognizes itself through common use of some jargonized expressions whose meaning is not clear to anyone, be it 'symbolic castration' or 'divided subject' – everyone refers to them, and what binds the group together is ultimately their very shared *ignorance*. Lacan's point, of course, is that psychoanalysis should enable the subject to *break* with this safe reliance on the enigmatic Master-Signifier.

- Secondly – and even more radically – when, in *Seminar XX: Encore*, Lacan developed the logic of 'non-all' and of the exception constitutive of the universal.[84] The paradox of the relationship between the series (of the elements belonging to the universal) and its exception does not lie only in the fact that 'the exception grounds the [universal] rule', that every universal series involves the exclusion of an exception (all men have inalienable rights – with the exception of madmen, criminals, primitives, the uneducated, children . . .). The properly dialectical point lies, rather, in the way a series and an exception *directly coincide*: the series is always the series of 'exceptions', of entities which display a certain exceptional quality that qualifies them to belong to the series (of heroes, of members of our community, of true citizens . . .). Recall the standard male seducer's list of female conquests: each of them is 'an exception', each was

> seduced for a particular *je ne sais quoi*, and the series is precisely the series of these exceptional figures. . . .[85]

This same matrix is also at work in the shifts of the Lacanian notion of the symptom. That is to say: what distinguishes the last stage of Lacan's teaching from the previous stages is best approached through the changed status of the notion of the symptom: previously, the symptom was a pathological formation to be (ideally, at least) dissolved in and through analytic interpretation: an indication that the subject somehow and somewhere compromised his desire, or an indication of the deficiency or malfunctioning of the symbolic Law that guarantees the subject's capacity to desire. In short, symptoms were the series of *exceptions*, of disturbances, malfunctionings, measured by the ideal of full integration into the symbolic Law, the big Other. Later, however, with his notion of the universalized symptom, Lacan accomplished the paradoxical shift from the 'masculine' logic of Law and its constitutive exception towards the 'feminine' logic in which there is *no* exception to the series of symptoms – in which there are *only* symptoms, and the symbolic Law (the paternal Name) is ultimately just one (the most efficient, the most established . . .) in the series of symptoms. This, according to Jacques-Alain Miller, is Lacan's universe in *Seminar XX*: a universe of radical split (between signifier and signified; between *jouissance* of drives and *jouissance* of the Other; between masculine and feminine) in which no a priori Law guarantees the connection or overlapping between the two sides, so that only partial and contingent knots–symptoms (quilting points, points of gravitation) can generate a limited and fragile co-ordination between the two domains. In this perspective, the 'dissolution of a symptom', far from bringing about the non-pathological state of full desiring capacity, leads, rather, to a total psychotic catastrophe, to the dissolution of the subject's entire universe.[86] There is no 'big Other' to guarantee the consistency of the symbolic space within which we dwell: there are only contingent, local and fragile points of stability.

The difference between these two notions of the symptom – the particular and the universalized ('*sinthome*') – accounts for the two opposed readings of the last shot of Hitchcock's *Vertigo* (Scottie standing at the precipice of the church tower, staring into the abyss into which Judy–Madeleine, his absolute love, vanished seconds ago): some interpreters see in it the indication of a happy ending (Scottie has finally got rid of his agoraphobia and is able fully to confront life), while others see in it utter despair (if Scottie survives the second loss of Judy–Madeleine, he will survive as a living dead). It all hinges on how we read Lacan's statement that 'woman is a symptom of man'. If we use the term 'symptom' in its traditional sense (a pathological formation which bears witness to the fact that the subject has betrayed his desire), then the final shot does imply a happy ending: Scottie's obsession with Madeleine was his 'symptom', the sign of his ethical weakness, so that when he gets rid of her, his rectitude is restored. If we use the term 'symptom' in its more radical sense, however – if Judy/Madeleine is his *sinthome* – then the final shot implies a catastrophic ending: when Scottie is deprived of his *sinthome*, his entire universe falls apart, loses its minimal consistency.

How does this shift, this undermining of the quasi-transcendental status of the big Other, affect *charity*? What survives this undermining is a charity much closer to the Christian meaning of this

SLAVOJ ŽIŽEK

term (this Christian charity is 'love', of which Lacan speaks in *Seminar XX*). So how is Davidson's semantic charity related to Christian charity? On a first approach, it may seem that they are to be opposed along the axis Imaginary–Symbolic: does not Christian charity operate at the level of imaginary compassion for our neighbour, with whom we identify, while Davidson's charity is clearly more formal, designating a purely symbolic (or, more precisely, semantic) function of trust, that is a priori presupposed in our communicative engagement? What, however, if there is another dimension at work in Christian charity, much closer to the dimension of the Other (subject) *qua* real? The key formal distinction between the two is that while semantic charity is a kind of a priori of language, formal and universal, always-already there, Christian charity is rare and fragile, something to be fought for and regained again and again. Even among Christians, confusion about its nature abounds. For that reason, perhaps the best way to define it is to proceed *a contrario*: to start by focusing on precisely those apparently Christian orientations which today threaten the proper Christian stance.

As is well known, the myth of the Grail is the exemplary case of religious-ideological 'ex-aptation' (to use the term developed by Stephen Jay Gould apropos of his criticism of orthodox Darwinism): it reinscribes into the Christian domain the pagan notion of a magical object that provides abundance and brings about seasonal rebirth and regeneration. In *Parsifal*, his last opera, Richard Wagner accomplishes the same process *backwards*: he interprets Christ's death and the Good Friday miracle as a pagan myth of seasonal death and rebirth. This gesture is profoundly anti-Christian: by breaking with the pagan notion of cosmic Justice and Balance, Christianity also breaks with the pagan notion of the circular death and rebirth of the Divinity – Christ's death is *not* the same as the seasonal death of the pagan god; rather, it designates a *rupture* with the circular movement of death and rebirth, the passage to a wholly different dimension of the Holy Spirit. One is tempted to claim that, for this reason, *Parsifal* is the model for all today's 'fundamentalist' Christians who, under the guise of returning to authentic Christian values, do precisely the opposite, and betray the subversive core of Christianity.

At what level does Christianity actually provide the foundation of human rights and freedoms? To put it in a somewhat simplified way, two basic attitudes are discernible in the history of religions, along the axis of the opposition between the *global* and the *universal*. On the one hand there is the pagan Cosmos, the Divine hierarchical order of cosmic Principles, which, applied to society, produces the image of a congruent edifice in which each member has its own place. Here the supreme Good is the global balance of Principles, while Evil stands for their derailment or derangement, for the excessive assertion of one Principle to the detriment of others (of the masculine Principle to the detriment of the feminine; of Reason to the detriment of Feeling . . .); the cosmic balance is then re-established through the work of Justice which, with its inexorable necessity, sets things straight again by crushing the derailed element. With regard to the social body, an individual is 'good' when he acts in accordance with his special place in the social edifice (when he respects Nature, which provides food and shelter; when he shows respect for his superiors, who take care of him in a fatherly way); and Evil occurs when some particular strata or individuals are no longer satisfied with this place (children no longer obey their parents, servants no longer obey their masters, the wise ruler turns into a capricious, cruel tyrant . . .). The very core of pagan Wisdom lies in its insight into this cosmic balance of hierarchically ordered Principles – more precisely, into the eternal circuit of the cosmic catastrophe (derailment) and the restoration of Order through just punishment. Perhaps the most elaborated case of such a cosmic order is the Ancient Hindu cosmology, applied first to the social order, in the guise of the caste system, and then to the individual organism itself, in the guise of the harmonious hierarchy of its organs (head, hands, abdomen . . .); today, such an attitude is artificially revived in the multitude of New Age approaches to nature and society.

Christianity (and, in its own way, Buddhism) introduced into this global balanced cosmic Order a principle that is totally foreign to it, a principle which, measured by the standards of pagan cosmology, cannot but appear as a monstrous distortion: the principle according to which each individual has *immediate* access to universality (of nirvana, of the Holy Spirit, or, today, of human Rights and freedoms): I can participate in this universal dimension *directly*, irrespective of my special place within the global social order. For that reason, Buddha's followers form a community of people who, in one way or another, have broken with the hierarchy of the social order and started to treat it as fundamentally *irrelevant*: in his choice of disciples, Buddha pointedly ignored castes and (after some hesitation, true) even sexual difference. And do not Christ's scandalous words from Saint Luke's Gospel point in the same direction: 'If anyone come to me and does not hate his father and his mother, his wife and children, his brothers and sisters – yes, even his own life – he cannot be my disciple' (14: 26)? Here, of course, we are *not* dealing with a simple brutal hatred demanded by a cruel and jealous God:

family relations stand here metaphorically for the entire socio-symbolic network, for any particular ethnic 'substance' that determines our place in the global Order of Things. The 'hatred' enjoined by Christ is not, therefore, a kind of pseudo-dialectical opposite to love, but a direct expression of what Saint Paul, in Corinthians I 13, with unsurpassable power, describes as *agape*, the key intermediary term between faith and hope: it is love itself that enjoins us to 'unplug' from the organic community into which we were born – or, as Paul puts it, for a Christian, there are neither men nor women, neither Jews nor Greeks. . . . No wonder that, for those fully identified with the Jewish 'national substance', as well as for the Greek philosophers and the proponents of the global Roman Empire, the appearance of Christ was a ridiculous and/or traumatic scandal.

We can see here how thoroughly heterogeneous is the Christian stance to that of pagan wisdom: in clear contrast to the ultimate horizon of pagan wisdom, the coincidence of opposites (the universe is the abyss of the primordial Ground in which all 'false' opposites – of Good and Evil, of appearance and reality, up to the very opposition between wisdom itself and the folly of being caught in the illusion of *maya* – coincide), Christianity asserts as the highest act precisely what pagan wisdom condemns as the source of Evil: the gesture of *separation*, of drawing the line, of clinging to an element that disturbs the balance of All. The pagan criticism that the Christian insight is not 'deep enough', that it fails to grasp the primordial One–All, therefore misses the point: Christianity *is* the miraculous Event that disturbs the balance of the One–All; it *is* the violent intrusion of Difference that precisely *throws the balanced circuit of the universe off the rails*.

From this standpoint, it would be interesting to approach the barely concealed ideological ambiguities of George Lucas's *Star Wars I: The Phantom Menace*, one of whose few points of interest as a film is the way it endeavours to outline the answer to the question of the 'origin of Evil': *how did Darth Vader become Darth Vader*, that is, how did Anakin Skywalker, this sweet boy, turn into the monstrous instrument of cosmic Evil? Two hints are crucial here: first, the 'Christological' features of the young Anakin (his mother hints that she became pregnant with him in an immaculate conception; the race he wins clearly echoes the famous chariot race in *Ben Hur*, this 'tale of Christ'); second, the fact that he is identified as the one who has the potential to 'restore the balance of the Force'. Since the ideological universe of *Star Wars* is the New Age pagan universe, it is quite significant that its central figure of Evil should echo Christ – within the pagan horizon, the Event of Christ *is* the ultimate scandal. Furthermore, what if – along Hegelian lines – we take the premonition that Anakin will 'restore the balance of the Force' not as the fateful misapprehension, but as a *correct* insight? What if the suffocating character of the pagan universe lay precisely in the fact that *it lacked the dimension of radical Evil* – that, in it, the balance was too much *in favour of the Good*? So the emergence of Christianity *did* in a way effectively 'restore the balance of the Force' precisely in so far as it *was* the intervention of radical Evil (the power of unheard-of negativity) that derailed the pallid and anaemic, self-satisfied, tolerant peaceful daily life of the late Roman Empire? Was this not – implicitly, at least – Schelling's thesis when, in *Weltalter*, he interpreted the emergence of Christ as the event of *Ent-Scheidung* (differentiating decision) which disturbs the balance of the pagan universe, of the vortex of its eternal circuit in which all differences are ultimately engulfed by the same abyss?

12 Christ's Uncoupling

It is precisely in order to emphasize this suspension of the social hierarchy that Christ (like Buddha before him) addresses in particular those who belong to the very bottom of the social hierarchy, the outcasts of the social order (beggars, prostitutes . . .) as the privileged and exemplary members of his new community. This new community is then explicitly constructed as a collective of outcasts, the antipode to any established 'organic' group. Perhaps the best way to imagine such a community is to locate it in the lineage of other 'eccentric' communities of outcasts that we know from past and present, from lepers and circus freaks to early computer hackers – groups in which stigmatized individuals are united by a secret bond of solidarity. In order to specify these communities further, one is tempted to risk the reference to Freud himself – in his *Crowd Psychology* he provides two examples of crowd formation: the Church and the Army. Usually, one takes them as equivalent, without considering the difference between the two. What, however, if this difference *is* crucial, along the lines of Laclau's opposition between the structure of differences and the antagonistic logic of equivalences? The Church is global: a structured Institution, an encompassing network of hierarchically differentiated positions, basically ecumenical, tolerant, prone to compromises, all-inclusive, dividing its spoils among its subgroups; while in the Army the emphasis is on antagonism, on Us versus Them, on egalitarian universalism (we are all ultimately equal when we are confronted with Them, the Enemy), so that the Army is ultimately exclusionary, prone to annihilate the other. Of course, this is a notional opposition: empirically, the line can well be blurred, and we often have a militant Church, or, on the contrary, an Army that functions as a Churchlike corporate social institution.

The fundamental paradox here is thus that with regard to empirical institutions, the two communities often exchange their proper places: it is the Church which is often close to the antagonistic functioning of the Army, and vice versa. Suffice it to recall the tension in the twelfth and thirteenth centuries between the Church *qua* institution and the emerging monastic orders as subversive counter-communities endangering the Church's established place within the social order, and all the difficulties the Church had in containing this excess and reinscribing this properly religious Event (such as the early movement founded by Saint Francis) within the confines of the order of Being. . . . Does not this opposition characterize the way Lacanians relate to the International Psycho-Analytical Association? The IPA is the psychoanalytic Church, excommunicating people from its ranks only when it feels actually threatened, prone to endless debates and compromises; Lacanians, on the contrary, are the psychoanalytic Army: a combative group working towards an aggressive reconquest, defined by the antagonism between Us and Them, avoiding and rejecting the tolerant olive branch of the IPA (come back, we accept you – but only if you also make a compromise and change slightly not the substance, but the form of your activity . . .). With regard to the political struggles, Freud's *wo es war, soll ich werden* can thus also be read as: where the Church was, the Army should arrive.

This is also the sense in which one should read those of Christ's statements which disrupt the circular logic of revenge or punishment destined to re-establish the balance of Justice: instead of 'An eye for an eye!', we get 'If someone slaps your right cheek, turn to him also your left cheek!' – the point here is not stupid masochism, humble acceptance of one's humiliation, but simply to *interrupt the circular logic of re-establishing balance.* It is interesting to observe how, even when Saint Paul does refer to the organicist metaphor of the religious community as a living body, he subverts it by turning it around: 'God has so arranged the body, giving the greater honour to the inferior member' (I Corinthians 12: 24) – that is to say, in the religious community, social hierarchy is reflected in an inverted way, so that the lowest deserve the greatest honour.

Of course, one should be careful here to avoid what psycho-analysis calls the perverse temptation: this 'unplugging' from the social body should not turn into perversion, in which we love the lowest outcast *because he is the lowest outcast* (thus secretly wanting him to *remain* so) – in this way, we do not actually 'unplug' from the hierarchic social order, but merely turn it around, set it on its head, and thus continue to parasitize on it (this perverse logic was brought to its extreme by the medieval sects whose members went so far as to eat the excrement of their fellow men in order to emphasize their compassionate solidarity even with the 'lowest in man'). And is not (on a different level, of course) a similar 'uncoupling' at work in passionate sexual love? Is not such love one of the greatest pulverizers of social hierarchy? When, in the balcony scene, Romeo and Juliet pathetically proclaim their renunciation and hatred of their own family names (Montague, Capulet), and thus 'unplug' themselves from their particular (family) social substance, do they not provide the supreme example of 'hatred of one's parents' as the direct expression of love? Furthermore, do we not encounter something similar in democratic 'unplugging': we are all directly members of the democratic collective, irrespective of our place in the intricate set of relations that form our respective communities?

Does not Christianity, however, go even a step further and enjoin us not only to hate our parents on behalf of the beloved one, but, in a dialectical inversion of love for one's enemy, 'to *hate the beloved* out of love and in love'?[87] The proper way to understand this is to ask a precise question: *what dimension* in the beloved other am I enjoined to hate? Let us take the hatred towards one's father in Oedipal family tension: as we see again and again, this hatred disappears, and a new understanding for the father emerges, the moment the son, in effect, gets rid of the shadow of paternal authority – in short, it disappears the moment the son perceives his father no longer as the embodiment of his socio-symbolic function, but as a vulnerable subject 'unplugged' from it. It is in this sense that, in true love, I 'hate the beloved out of love': I 'hate' the dimension of his inscription into the socio-symbolic structure on behalf of my very love for him as a unique person. However, to avoid a crucial misunderstanding that might arise here: this 'unplugging' of *agape* has nothing whatsoever to do with the common 'humanist' idea that one should forget about 'artificial' symbolic predicates and perceive one's neighbours in their unique humanity, that is, see the 'real human person' beneath their 'social roles', their ideological mandates and masks – here Saint Paul is quite firm in his 'theoretical anti-humanism':

> From now on, therefore, we regard no one from a human point of view; even though we once knew Christ from a human point of view, we know him no longer in that way. So if anyone is in Christ, there is a new creation: everything old has passed away; see, everything has become new! (II Corinthians 5: 16–17)

In this 'uncoupling', the neighbour is thus reduced to a singular member of the community of believers (of the 'Holy Ghost') – to use the Althusserian–Lacanian opposition, it is not the symbolic subject who is reduced to the 'real' individual, it is the individual (in all the wealth of his 'personality') who is reduced to the *singular point of subjectivity*; as such, 'uncoupling' does actually involve a 'symbolic death' – one has to 'die for the law' (Saint Paul) that regulates our tradition, our social 'substance'. The term 'new creation' is revealing here, signalling the gesture of *sublimation*, of erasing the traces of one's past ('everything old has passed away') and beginning afresh from a zero-point: consequently, there is also a terrifying *violence* at work in this 'uncoupling', that of the *death drive*, of the radical 'wiping the slate clean' as the condition of the New Beginning.

Such an 'unplugging' as the direct expression of love has nothing whatsoever to do with the escape into an idealized Romantic universe in which all concrete social differences magically disappear – to quote Kierkegaard again: '*love believes everything – and yet is never to be deceived*',[88] in contrast to the mistrust which believes nothing and is nevertheless thoroughly deceived. The person who mistrusts his others is, paradoxically, in his very cynical disbelief, the victim of the most radical self-deception: as Lacan would have put it, *les non-dupes errent* – the cynic misses the efficiency/actuality of the appearance itself, however fleeting, fragile and elusive it is; while the true believer believes in appearances, in the magic dimension that 'shines through' an appearance – he sees Goodness in the other where the other himself is not aware of it. Here appearance and reality are no longer opposed: precisely in trusting appearances, a loving person sees the other the way she/he effectively is, and loves her for her very foibles, not despite them. With regard to this point, the Oriental notion of the Absolute Void–Substance–Ground beneath the fragile, deceptive appearances that constitute our reality is to be opposed to the notion that it is the ordinary reality that is hard, inert, stupidly there, and the Absolute that is thoroughly fragile and fleeting. That is to say: what *is* the Absolute? Something that appears to us in fleeting experiences – say, through the gentle smile of a beautiful woman, or even through the warm, caring smile of a person who may otherwise seem ugly and rude: in such miraculous but *extremely fragile* moments, another dimension transpires through our reality. As such, the Absolute is easily corroded; it slips all too easily through our fingers, and must be handled as carefully as a butterfly.

In Lacanian terms, the difference here is the one between *idealization* and *sublimation*: false idolizing idealizes, it blinds itself to the other's weaknesses – or, rather, it blinds itself to the other *as such*, using the beloved as a blank screen on to which it projects its own phantasmagorical constructions; while true love accepts the beloved the way she or he is, merely putting her/him into the place of the Thing, the unconditional Object. As every true Christian knows, love is the *work* of love – the hard and arduous work of repeated 'uncoupling' in which, again and again, we have to disengage ourselves from the inertia that constrains us to identify with the particular order we were born into. Through the Christian work of compassionate love, we discern in what was hitherto a disturbing foreign body, tolerated and even modestly supported by us so that we were not too bothered by it, a subject, with its crushed dreams and desires – it is *this* Christian heritage of 'uncoupling' that is threatened by today's 'fundamentalisms', especially when they proclaim themselves Christian. Does not Fascism ultimately involve the return to the pagan mores which, rejecting the love of one's enemy, cultivate full identification with one's own ethnic community?

We are now also in a position to answer the ultimate counterargument: is it not that Christianity none the less supports participation in the social game (obey the laws of the country, even if your ultimate fidelity is to God), and thus generates ideal subjects of the existing order? In other words, is not the Christian 'uncoupling' ultimately the same as the old Hindu 'action with an inner distance' (the virtue of accomplishing acts with an indifference towards their goal) from the *Bhaghavad-Gita*, as the following passage seems to imply:

> the appointed time has grown short; from now on, let even those who have wives be as though they had none, and those who mourn as though they were not mourning, and those who rejoice as though they were not rejoicing, and those who buy as though they had no possessions, and those who deal with the world as though they had no dealings with it. For the present form of this world is passing away. (I Corinthians 7: 29–31)

The answer is that the Christian 'unplugging' is *not* an inner contemplative stance, but the active *work* of love which necessarily leads to the creation of an *alternative* community. Furthermore, in clear contrast to the Fascist carnivalesque 'unplugging' from the established symbolic rules, which functions as the inherent transgression of the existing order, *the proper Christian uncoupling suspends not so much the explicit laws but, rather, their implicit spectral obscene supplement.*

13   'You must, because you can!'

Let us specify this crucial point by reference to a well-known tasteless defence of Hitler: 'True, Hitler did some horrible things, like trying to rid Germany of Jews, but we should not forget that he none the less did some good things, like building highways and making the trains run on time!' The whole point of this defence, of course, is that although it formally denounces anti-Semitic violence, it is covertly anti-Semitic: the very gesture of comparing the anti-Semitic horrors to building highways, and putting them together in a statement whose structure is that of 'Yes, I know, but none the less . . .', makes it clear that praising Hitler's construction of highways is a displaced way of praising his anti-Semitic measures. The proof is that the critique of Hitler which *turns around* the terms of the first one (popular in some extremely conservative ecological circles) is no less acceptable, but implies an even stronger *defence* of Hitler, albeit in the form of criticism: 'True, Hitler did some good things, like trying to rid Germany of Jews, but we should not forget that he none the less did some horrible things, like building highways and thus ruining Germany's environment . . .'. And is not a similar reversal also the true content of the standard defence of the perpetrators of extreme-Right racist violence:

'True, he did participate in lynchings of African-Americans, but we should not forget that he was also a good and honest family man who went regularly to church . . .' – instead of this, one should read: 'True, he did do some good things, like trying to get rid of the nasty African-Americans; none the less, we should not forget that he was just a common family man who went regularly to church . . .'. The key to this reversal is that in both cases we are dealing with the tension between the publicly acknowledged and acceptable ideological content (building highways, going to church) and its obscene disavowed underside (Holocaust, lynchings): the first, standard, version of the statement acknowledges the public content and disavows its obscene underside (while secretly endorsing it); the second version openly dismisses the public aspect and endorses the obscene underside.

So, in so far as, with regard to the duality of 'official' public symbolic narrative space and its spectral double, the public symbolic space is regulated by the symbolic Law, what kind of law is operative in the uncanny domain of its spectral double? The answer, of course, is: *superego*.[89] One should bear in mind here that the tension between the symbolic Law and the impossible/real Thing access to which is prohibited by the Law (ultimately, the maternal Thing prohibited by the paternal Law) is not Lacan's ultimate horizon – what lies beyond (or, rather, beneath) it is the uncanny Thing which itself 'makes the Law':

> *Das Ding* presents itself at the level of unconscious experience as that which already makes the law. . . . It is a capricious and arbitrary law, the law of the oracle, the law of signs in which the subject receives no guarantee from anywhere.[90]

So we no longer have *das Ding* as the dark *beyond*, constituted by the prohibitory Law: the ultimate horror is that of the real Thing itself which directly 'makes the law'. And in so far as the Thing stands for *jouissance*, this Law which is the Law of the Thing itself is, of course, none other than the superego, the law whose injunction is the impossible command 'Enjoy!'. This is also the dimension that is the obverse of the Kantian logic of the infinite approach to the impossible goal: in Kant's horizon, the Thing remains inaccessible, a void beyond the Law, while the Law–Thing displays as it were the Sadeian obverse/truth of Kant, a perverse Law that is the Law of the Thing itself.

The superego suspension of moral prohibitions is the crucial feature of today's 'postmodern' nationalism. Here, the cliché according to which passionate ethnic identification restores a firm set of values and beliefs in the confusing insecurity of a modern secular global society is to be turned around: nationalist 'fundamentalism' serves, rather, as the operator of a secret, barely concealed *You may*! It is today's apparently hedonistic and permissive postmodern reflexive society which is paradoxically more and more saturated by rules and regulations that allegedly promote our well-being (restrictions on smoking and eating, rules against sexual harassment . . .), so that the reference to some passionate ethnic identification, far from further restraining us, functions rather as the liberating call 'You may!' – you may violate (not the Decalogue, but) the rigid regulations of peaceful coexistence in a liberal tolerant society; you may eat and drink whatever you like; engage in patriarchal mores prohibited by liberal Political Correctness; even hate, fight, kill and rape. . . . Without the full recognition of this perverse pseudo-liberating effect of today's nationalism – of how the obscenely permissive superego supplements the explicit texture of the social-symbolic law – we condemn ourselves to a failure to grasp its true dynamics.[91] This is how Aleksandar Tijanić, a leading Serb columnist who was for a brief period even Milošević's Minister for Information and Public Media, describes 'the strange kind of symbiosis between Milošević and the Serbs':

> Milošević generally suits the Serbs. In the time of his rule, Serbs abolished the time for working. No one does anything. He allowed the flourishing of the black market and smuggling. You can appear on state TV and insult Blair, Clinton, or anyone else of the 'world dignitaries'. . . . Furthermore, Milošević gave us the right to carry weapons. He gave us the right to solve all our problems with weapons. He gave us also the right to drive stolen cars. . . . Milošević changed the daily life of Serbs into one great holiday and enabled us all to feel like high-school pupils on a graduation trip – which means that nothing, but really nothing, of what you do can be punishable.[92]

The superego is thus the properly obscene reversal of the permissive 'You may!' into the prescriptive 'You must!', the point at which permitted enjoyment turns into ordained enjoyment. We all know Kant's formula of the unconditional ethical imperative *Du kannst, denn du sollst! (You can [do your duty] because you must [do it]!*; the superego inverts this Kantian *You can, because you must!* into *You should [you must], because you can!*. Nowhere is this clearer than in the case of the unfortunate Viagra, the potency pill that promises to restore the capacity of male erection in a purely biochemical way, bypassing all problems with psychological inhibitions: now that Viagra takes care of the erection, there is no excuse: you should enjoy sex; if you don't it's your fault! At the opposite end of the spectrum, the New Age wisdom of recovering the spontaneity of your true Self seems to offer a way out of this superego predicament – what, however, do we actually find there? Is this New Age attitude of wisdom not again secretly sustained by the superego imperative: 'You must [do your duty of achieving your full self-realization and self-fulfilment], because you can!'? Is this not why we often feel a real terroristic pressure beneath the compliant tolerance of New Age preachers?[93] To put it in somewhat simplified terms: the elementary authoritarian 'wisdom' is that man is a weak, corrupted being who needs a strong Master to control his dangerous antisocial impulses; this is why the traditional *authoritarian* Master tells us: 'No matter what you think deep in yourself, no matter how difficult and against your nature you find it, *obey* [my orders], repress and renounce your inner urges!'; the *totalitarian* Master's message in contrast is: 'I know better than you do yourself what you *really want*, what is in your best interests, so what I order you to do is what you, deep within yourself, really unknowingly desire, even if you seem superficially to be opposed to it!'

This external opposition between 'pleasure and duty' can be overcome in two ways. On the one hand, we have the paradox of the extremely oppressive 'totalitarian' power which goes even further than traditional 'authoritarian' power – it does not only tell you: 'Do your duty; I don't care if you like it or not!', it tells you: 'Not only must you obey my orders and do your duty, you must do it with pleasure, you must enjoy doing it!' (This is how totalitarian populist democracy works: it is not enough for the subjects to follow their Leader, they must actively *love* him . . .). On the other hand, we have the obverse paradox of the pleasure whose very pursuit turns into duty: in a 'permissive' society, subjects experience the need to 'have a good time', really to enjoy themselves, as a kind of duty; consequently, they feel guilty if they fail to be happy. . . . And my point is that the concept of the superego designates precisely the interzone in which these two opposites overlap: in which the command to *enjoy doing your duty* overlaps with the *duty to enjoy yourself.*

Here, again, the role of Christianity is ambiguous: 'You have heard that it was said, "You shall not commit adultery." But I say to you that everyone who looks at a woman with lust has already committed adultery with her in his heart' (Matthew 5: 27–8). Does this gesture of going a step further with regard to the Decalogue, and prohibiting not only sinful deeds but sinful thoughts themselves, designate the shift from the Jewish symbolic Prohibition to its superego elaboration (not only should you not *act* upon your sinful desires, you should fight them – these desires themselves, even if you successfully resist them, are already equivalent to committing the sin, so you should renounce/transform your desires themselves, and desire only what is permitted)? Or does Christianity, on the contrary, endeavour to break the very vicious cycle of prohibition that generates the desire to transgress it, the cycle described by Saint Paul in Romans 7: 7?

14   From Knowledge to Truth . . . and Back

Let us approach this dilemma from another perspective, that of the dialectical tension between Knowledge and Truth. Usually, psychoanalysis operates in the domain of the opposition between factual 'objective' knowledge and 'subjective' truth: one can lie in the guise of truth (this is what obsessionals are doing when, in statements which are factually entirely accurate, they conceal or disavow their desire); one can tell the truth in the guise of a lie (the hysterical procedure, or a simple slip of the tongue which betrays the subject's true desire). In *Darwin's Dangerous Idea*, Daniel Dennett evokes the following mental experiment: You and your best friend are about to be captured by hostile forces, who speak English but do not know much about your world. You both know Morse code, and hit upon the following impromptu encryption scheme: for a dash, tell the truth; for a dot, lie. Your captors, of course, listen to you talking to each other: 'Birds lay eggs, and toads fly. Chicago is a city, and my feet are not made of tin, and baseball is played in August,' you say, answering 'No' (dash–dot; dash–dash–dash) to whatever your friend has just asked. Even if your captors know Morse code, unless they can determine the truth and falsity of these sentences, they cannot detect the properties that stand for dot and dash.[94] Dennett himself uses this example to make the point that meaning cannot be accounted for in purely inherent syntactic terms: the only way ultimately to gain access to the meaning of a statement is to situate it in its lifeworld context, that is, to take into account its semantic dimension, the objects and processes to which it refers. My point is rather different: as Dennett himself puts it, in this case, the two prisoners use the world itself as a 'one-time pad' – although the truth-value of their statements is not indifferent but crucial, it is not this truth-value as such, in itself, that matters; what matters is the translation of truth-value into a differential series of pluses and minuses (dashes and dots) which delivers the true message in Morse code.

Does not something similar also go on in the psychoanalytic process? Although the truth-value of the patient's statements is not indifferent, what really matters is not this truth-value as such, but the way the very alternation of truths and lie discloses the patient's desire – a patient also uses reality itself (the way he relates to it) as a 'one-time pad' to encrypt his desire. When a patient claims that she has been molested by her father, one should, of course, establish if this harassment really took place or not; what ultimately matters, however, is not this harassment as such, but the role it plays in the patient's symbolic economy, the way it was 'subjectivized'. If we learn that the act of harassment did *not* take place in reality, then the fact that the patient fantasizes intensely about it acquires a different symbolic value, while still telling us a lot about her desire.

However, this notion of authentic subjective Truth as opposed to mere 'objective' knowledge is not Lacan's last word. In Lacan's late work there is a certain knowledge (equivalent to drive) more fundamental than (subjective) Truth itself. At the Lacanian conference *The Subject – Encore* at UCLA in March 1999, one of the participants discussed a recent medico-legal case of a woman who, on religious grounds, unconditionally rejected the transfusion that would have saved her life. The judge before whom she was brought asked her: 'What if you were to be submitted to transfusion *against your will*? Would this also condemn you to damnation and hell in your afterlife, or not?' After a brief deliberation, the woman answered: 'I guess the answer is no.' When he heard this, the judge took the responsibility upon himself: in order to save the woman's life without putting her in an unbearable moral predicament, he proclaimed her irresponsible, and ordered the transfusion against her will. What is the ethical status of this decision?

The participants hailed the judge's intervention as a model of the inventive approach. Such an approach can also serve as a prototype of a successful analyst's intervention: how to enable the patient to assert his fundamental will-to-life without harming his ideological and symbolic identifications. From the standpoint of psychoanalytic ethics, however, such a solution is *false*. It is a neat practical solution – in the judge's position I would probably do the same thing – but it does not force the subject to confront the truth of her desire. Rather, it involves the helpful-compassionate procedure of proposing a beneficial protective fiction – or, to put it somewhat bluntly, of a *lie*. Because ultimately, this solution *is* a lie: when the poor woman was asked: 'What if you were to be submitted to transfusion *against your will*? Would this also condemn you to damnation and hell in your afterlife, or not?', *she knew perfectly well that if she answered 'No', the judge would order enforced transfusion*. To make the fact that the choice of having a transfusion or not was actually in her own hands clear, one should introduce here the Lacanian distinction between the subject of statement and the subject of enunciation: by answering truthfully on the level of *statement* (she truly believed that enforced transfusion does not count as a mortal sin), she sinned (she lied and endorsed transfusion) on the level of her subjective position of *enunciation* – that is to say, the true content of her 'no' was 'yes, please, do give me a transfusion' (like the proverbial male chauvinist figure of a hypocritical woman who can enjoy sex only if she is half forced into it, so that she can pretend that it is happening to her against her will). So, again, paradoxically, the only way for her to be *true to herself* on the level of subjective Truth (the position of enunciation) would have been to *lie* at the level of statement – to answer 'Yes!' even if she really thought that transfusion against one's will is not a mortal sin – only in this way could she have prevented the transfusion.

Does this alternative, however, really cover all the options? Is it not possible to imagine the poor woman answering accurately (the way she did: 'No') *without* sinning? What if we simply imagine a subject who escapes the tension between objective knowledge and subjective Truth by suspending the very dimension of Truth, and sticking to cold impersonal Knowledge? That is to say: what if the poor woman were to answer 'No' not in order secretly to save herself, but out of a radical *disregard* for subjective consequences? (In this case, it would be totally inappropriate to claim that the judge, as a good analyst, detected in her a disavowed desire to live, and gently, through the beneficial lie, allowed her to realize this desire without breaking her religious code.) Here, one should recall Jacques-Alain Miller's precise point that the aim of analytic discourse is to practise a language which *does not deceive* or conceal, does not use its direct meaning as part of some hidden rhetorical strategy of argumentation. Oswald Ducrot[95] developed the thesis that in our language all predicates are ultimately just reified argumentative procedures – in the last resort, we use language not to designate some reality, some content, but to dupe the other, to win an argument, to seduce or threaten, to conceal our true desire. . . . In ordinary language, the truth is never fully established; there are always pros and cons; for each argument there are counter-arguments; there is 'another side' to every point; every statement can be negated; undecidability is all-encompassing – this eternal vacillation is interrupted only by the intervention of some quilting point (Master-Signifier). According to Lacan, however, psychoanalytic discourse is part of modern science in that it aims at breaking this vicious cycle of all-pervasive argumentation, but *not* in the mode of the quilting point: the signifiers do not need such a point in order to be stabilized because they are already, in their very functioning, not vacillating, not caught in the eternal sliding of meaning.

So, on this level, the subject breaks out of the vicious cycle of interpretation – her 'No!' is no longer to be interpreted, since what she actually desires is simply *irrelevant*. And maybe this is also the way to answer the standard Christian criticism that the Jews, by seeking ways of obeying God's commandments and prohibitions literally, while none the less retaining what they desire, in effect cheat Him. (There is a religious institution in Israel which deals specifically with issues of how to circumvent prohibitions; significantly enough, it is called *The Institute for Judaism and Science*.) This criticism is meaningful within the confines of the standard Christian attitude where what matters is the spirit, not the letter – where you are guilty if the desire was in your heart, even if you did not break any letter of the law by your deeds. When, in order not to break the injunction that no pigs should be raised on the holy land of Israel, pigs are raised today on plateaus three feet above the ground, the Christian interpretation would be: 'See how hypocritical the Jews are! The meaning of their God's command is clear – simply do not raise pigs! And the Jews, in a profoundly hypocritical way, take the Divine statement *literally*, focusing on the totally unimportant specification "on the land of Israel", and thus find a way of violating the spirit of the injunction, while keeping to its letter. For us Christians, they are already guilty in their hearts, because they spend all their energy not on internalizing God's prohibition, but on how to have their cake and eat it, that is, on how to circumvent the prohibition.'

The answer to this would be simply to suspend the entire domain of interpretation: what if the poor woman, in answering 'No', was *not* hypocritically counting on the fact that her desire to live would be fulfilled, that she would get her transfusion, without being responsible for it, and thus having to pay the price for it? What if her stance was, rather, that of radical *indifference* towards the entire domain of the possible pathological (in the Kantian sense of the term) effects of telling the truth? What if her implicit ethical axiom was the exact inversion of the standard 'You should tell the truth, even if it hurts you!' – 'You should tell the truth, *even if it helps you*!'? The fundamental lesson of the psychoanalytic notion of superego is that – *pace* the neoconservatives who bemoan the allegedly hedonistic narcissism of our age – there are few things more difficult than to enjoy, without guilt, the fruits of doing one's duty (in this case, the duty of telling the truth). While it is easy to enjoy acting in an egotistic way *against* one's duty, it is, perhaps, only as the result of psychoanalytic treatment that one can acquire the capacity to enjoy *doing* one's duty; perhaps this *is* one of the definitions of the end of psychoanalysis.

One can easily see how this solution enables us to break the vicious cycle of the superego: the Christian logic of 'even if you only thought of it, you are already as guilty as if you had committed the act' relies on the guilt feeling; it involves the superego paradox of 'the more you repress your transgressive desire in order to obey the Law, the more this desire returns in your thoughts and obsesses you; consequently, the guiltier you are'. From this Christian perspective, of course, the Jewish literal obedience to the Law cannot but appear as the ultimate opportunistic manipulation which implies a totally external relationship towards the Law as the set of rules to be tweaked so that one can nevertheless achieve one's true aim – what bothers Christians is the fact that the Jews do not see the cheap trickery of their procedure, so that when they succeed in having their cake and eating it, in realizing their goal without disobeying the letter of the Law, they *do not feel any guilt*. But what if this lack of guilt demonstrates precisely that the Christian criticism according to which the Jews cheaply manipulate the Law without renouncing their pathological goals misses the point: I can tell the truth without guilt, even if it helps me, because *it is only truth that matters*, not my desires invested in it. So, far from being the 'religion of guilt', the Jewish religion precisely enables us to avoid guilt – it is Christianity that manipulates guilt much more effectively.[96]

The superego dialectic of Law and transgression does not lie only in the fact that Law itself invites its own transgression, that it generates the desire for its own violation; our obedience to the Law itself is not 'natural', spontaneous, but *always-already mediated by the (repression of the) desire to transgress the Law*. When we obey the Law, we do so as part of a desperate strategy to fight against our desire to transgress it, so the more rigorously we *obey* the Law, the more we bear witness to the fact that, deep within ourselves, we feel the pressure of the desire to indulge in sin. The superego feeling of guilt is therefore right: the more we obey the Law, the more we *are* guilty, because this obedience, in effect, *is* a defence against our sinful desire; and in Christianity, the *desire* (intention) to sin equals the *act* itself – if you simply covet your neighbour's wife, you are already committing adultery. This

Christian superego attitude is perhaps best expressed by T.S. Eliot's line from *Murder in the Cathedral*: 'the highest form of treason: to do the right thing for the wrong reason' – even when you do the right thing, you do it in order to counteract, and thus conceal, the basic vileness of your true nature. . . . It is *this* superego dialectic that is successfully avoided by the Jews: *their* obedience to the Law is not mediated by the repressed desire to sin, which is why they can stick to the letter of the Law and none the less find ways of realizing their desire without any guilt feelings. . . . However, this superego dialectic of the transgressive desire engendering guilt is *not* the ultimate horizon of Christianity: as Saint Paul makes clear, the Christian stance, at its most radical, involves precisely the suspension of the vicious cycle of Law and its transgressive desire. How are we to resolve this deadlock?

15 The Breakout

Our answer is that the passage from Judaism to Christianity ultimately obeys the matrix of the passage from the 'masculine' to the 'feminine' formulae of sexuation. Let us clarify this passage apropos of the opposition between the *jouissance* of drives and the *jouissance* of the Other, elaborated by Lacan in *Seminar XX: Encore*; this opposition is also sexualized according to the same matrix. On the one hand we have the closed, ultimately solipsistic, circuit of drives which find their satisfaction in idiotic masturbatory (autoerotic) activity, in the perverse circulating around *objet petit a* as the object of a drive. On the other hand, there are subjects for whom access to *jouissance* is much more closely linked to the domain of the Other's discourse, to how they not so much talk, as are talked about: say, erotic pleasure hinges on the seductive talk of the lover, on the satisfaction provided by the speech itself, not just on the act in its stupidity. And does not this contrast explain the long-observed difference in how the two sexes relate to cyberspace sex? Men are much more prone to use cyberspace as a masturbatory device for their solitary playing, immersed in stupid repetitive pleasure, while women are more prone to participate in chatrooms, using cyberspace for seductive exchanges of speech.

Do we not encounter a clear case of this opposition between the masculine phallic/masturbatory *jouissance* of the drive and the feminine *jouissance* of the Other in Lars von Trier's film *Breaking the Waves*? Crippled and confined to his hospital bed, Jan tells his wife Bess that she must make love to other men and describe her experiences to him in detail – in this way, she will keep his will-to-life alive: although she will be performing the act physically with other men, the true sex will occur in their conversation. . . . Jan's *jouissance* is clearly phallic/masturbatory: he uses Bess to provide him with the fantasmatic screen he needs in order to be able to indulge in solipsistic masturbatory *jouissance*, while Bess finds *jouissance* on the level of the Other (symbolic order), that is, in her words – for her the ultimate source of satisfaction is not the sexual acts themselves (she commits them in a purely mechanical way, as a necessary sacrifice) but the way she *reports* on them to Jan. More precisely, Bess's *jouissance* is that 'of the Other' in more than one sense of the term: enjoyment not only in words, but also (and this is ultimately just another aspect of the thing) in the sense of utter alienation – her enjoyment is totally alienated/externalized in Jan as her Other; that is, it lies entirely in her awareness that she is enabling the Other to enjoy. (This example is crucial in so far as it enables us to dispense with the standard misreading of Lacan according to which *jouissance féminine* is a mystical beatitude beyond speech, exempted from the symbolic order – quite on the contrary, it is the woman who is immersed into the order of speech *without exception*.)[97]

So how does all this allow us to throw a new light on the tension between Judaism and Christianity? The first paradox to note is that the vicious dialectic of Law and its transgression elaborated by Saint Paul is the invisible third term, the 'vanishing mediator' between the Jewish religion and Christianity – its spectre haunts both of them, although neither of the two religious positions actually occupies its place: on the one hand, the Jews are *not yet* there, that is, they treat the Law as the written Real which does not engage them in the vicious superego cycle of guilt; on the other, as Saint Paul makes clear, the basic point of Christianity proper is precisely to *break out* of the vicious superego cycle of the Law and its transgression via Love. In his Seminar on the *Ethics of Psychoanalysis*, Lacan deals extensively with the Pauline dialectic of the Law and its transgression – perhaps one should therefore read this Pauline dialectic together with its corollary, Saint Paul's *other* paradigmatic passage, the one on love from I Corinthians 13:

> If I speak in the tongues of mortals and of angels, but do not have love, I am a noisy gong or a clanging cymbal. And if I have prophetic powers, and understand all mysteries and all knowledge, and if I have all faith, so as to remove mountains, but do not have love, I am nothing. If I give away all my possessions, and if I hand over my body so that I may boast

[alternative translation: to be burned], but do not have love, I gain nothing. . . . Love never ends. But as for prophecies, they will come to an end; as for tongues, they will cease; as for knowledge, it will come to an end. For we know only in part, and we prophesy only in part; but when the complete comes, the partial will come to an end. . . . For now we see in a mirror, dimly, but then we will see face to face. Now I know only in part; then I will know fully, even as I have been fully known. And now faith, hope, and love abide, these three; and the greatest of these is love.

Crucial here is the clearly paradoxical place of Love with regard to All (to the *completed* series of knowledge or prophecies). First, Saint Paul claims that love is there even if we possess *all* knowledge – then, in the second part of the passage, he claims that love is there only for *incomplete* beings, that is, beings who possess incomplete knowledge. When I 'know fully . . . as I have been fully known', will there still be love? Although, in contrast to knowledge, 'love never ends', it is clearly only 'now' (while I am still incomplete) that 'faith, hope, and love abide'. The only way out of this deadlock is to read the two inconsistent claims according to Lacan's *feminine* formulae of sexuation: even when it is 'all' (complete, with no exception), the field of knowledge remains in a way non-all, incomplete – love is not an exception to the All of knowledge, but precisely that 'nothing' which makes even the complete series/field of knowledge incomplete. In other words, the point of the claim that even if I were to possess all knowledge, without love I would be nothing, is not simply that *with* love, I am 'something' – in love, *I am also nothing* but, as it were, a Nothing humbly aware of itself, a Nothing paradoxically made rich through the very awareness of its lack. Only a lacking, vulnerable being is capable of love: the ultimate mystery of love is therefore that incompleteness is in a way *higher than completion*. On the one hand, only an imperfect, lacking being loves: we love because we do *not* know all. On the other hand, even if we were to know everything, love would inexplicably still be higher than completed knowledge. Perhaps the true achievement of Christianity is to elevate a loving (imperfect) Being to the place of God – that is, of ultimate perfection. Lacan's extensive discussion of love in *Encore* should thus be read in the Pauline sense, as opposed to the dialectic of the Law and its transgression: this second dialectic is clearly 'masculine'/phallic; it involves the tension between the All (the universal Law) and its constitutive exception; while love is 'feminine', it involves the paradoxes of the non-All.

Consequently, there are two ways of subverting the Law, the 'masculine' and the 'feminine'. One can *violate/transgress its prohibitions*: this is the inherent transgression which sustains the Law, like the advocates of liberal democracy who secretly (through the CIA) train murderers-terrorists for the proto-Fascist regimes in Latin America. That is false rightist heroism: secretly doing the 'necessary but dirty thing', that is, violating the explicit ruling ideology (of human Rights, and so on) in order to sustain the existing order. Much more subversive than this is *simply to do what is allowed*, that is, what the existing order explicitly allows, although it prohibits it at the level of implicit unwritten prohibitions. In short – to paraphrase Brecht's well-known crack about how mild robbing a bank is in comparison with founding a bank – how mild transgressing the Law is in comparison with *obeying it thoroughly* – or, as Kierkegaard put it, in his unique way:

'We do not laud the son who said "No," but we endeavour to learn from the gospel how dangerous it is to say, "Sir, I will."'[98] What better example is there than Hašek's immortal 'good soldier Schweik', who caused total havoc in the old Imperial Austrian Army simply by obeying orders all too literally? (Although, strictly speaking, there *is* a better example, namely the 'absolute example' [Hegel], Christ himself: when Christ claims that he is here merely to *fulfil* the [Jewish] Law, he thereby bears witness to how his act effectively *cancels* the Law.)

The basic paradox of the relationship between public power and its inherent transgression is that *the subject is actually 'in' (caught in the web of) power only and precisely in so far as he does not fully identify with it but maintains a kind of distance towards it*; on the other hand, the system (of public Law) is actually undermined by unreserved identification with it. Stephen King's 'Rita Hayworth and the Shawshank Redemption' tackles this problem with due stringency apropos of the paradoxes of prison life. The cliché about prison life is that I am actually integrated into it, ruined by it, when my accommodation to it is so overwhelming that I can no longer stand or even imagine freedom, life outside prison, so that my release brings about a total psychic breakdown, or at least gives rise to a longing for the lost safety of prison life. The actual dialectic of prison life, however, is somewhat more refined. Prison in effect destroys me, attains a total hold over me, precisely when I do *not* fully consent to the fact that I am in prison but maintain a kind of inner distance towards it, stick to the illusion that 'real life is elsewhere' and indulge all the time in daydreaming about life outside, about nice things that are waiting for me after my release or escape. I thereby get caught in the vicious cycle of fantasy, so that when, eventually, I am released, the grotesque discord between fantasy and reality breaks me down. The only true solution is therefore fully to accept the rules of prison life and then, within the universe governed by these rules, to work out a way to beat them. In short, inner distance and daydreaming about Life Elsewhere in effect enchain me to prison, whereas full acceptance of the fact that I am really there, bound by prison rules, opens up a space for true hope.

What this means is that in order effectively to liberate oneself from the grip of existing social reality, one should first renounce the transgressive fantasmatic supplement that attaches us to it. In what does this renunciation consist? In a series of recent (commercial) films, we find the same surprising radical gesture. In *Speed*, when the hero (Keanu Reeves) is confronting the terrorist blackmailer who is holding his partner at gunpoint, the hero shoots not the blackmailer, but *his own partner* in the leg – this apparently senseless act momentarily shocks the blackmailer, who releases the hostage and runs away. . . . In *Ransom*, when the media tycoon (Mel Gibson) goes on television to answer the kidnappers' request for two million dollars as a ransom for his son, he surprises everyone by saying that he will offer two million dollars to anyone who will give him any information about the kidnappers, and announces that he will pursue them to the end, with all his resources, if they do not release his son immediately. This radical gesture not only stuns the kidnappers – immediately after accomplishing it, Gibson himself almost breaks down, aware of the risk he is courting. . . . And, finally, the supreme case: when, in the flashback scene from *The Usual Suspects*, the mysterious Keyser Soeze returns home and finds his wife and small daughter held at gunpoint by the members of a rival mob, he resorts to the radical gesture of shooting his wife and daughter themselves dead – this act enables him mercilessly to pursue members of the rival gang, their families, parents and friends, killing them all. . . . What these three gestures have in common is that in a situation of forced choice, the subject makes the 'crazy', impossible choice of, in a way, *striking at himself*, at what is most precious to himself. This act, far from amounting to a case of impotent aggressivity turned against oneself, rather changes the co-ordinates of the situation in which the subject finds himself: by cutting himself loose from the precious object through whose possession the enemy kept him in check, the subject gains the space of free action. Is not such a radical gesture of 'striking at oneself' constitutive of subjectivity as such?

Was not such a gesture already that of Abraham, commanded by God to sacrifice Isaac, his only son, that which mattered more to him than himself? In his case, of course, an angel intervened at the last moment, staying Abraham's hand. (In the Christian reading, one could claim that the actual killing was unnecessary, since the only thing that mattered was inner intention, just as one has already committed a sin if one simply covets one's neighbour's wife.) But here, precisely, we can draw the line that separates the classical hero from the modern hero: if Abraham were a modern hero, no angel would appear at the last moment; he would actually have to slaughter his son. And – closer to our own time – is not such a gesture also the crux of Freud's late book *Moses and Monotheism*? How did he react to the Nazi anti-Semitic threat? Not by joining the ranks of the beleaguered Jews in the defence of their legacy, but by targeting his own people, the most precious part of the Jewish legacy, the founding figure of Moses – that is, by endeavouring to deprive the Jews of this figure, proving that Moses was not a Jew at all: in this way, he effectively undermined the very unconscious foundation of anti-Semitism. Furthermore, did not Lacan himself accomplish a similar act of 'shooting at himself' when, in 1979, he dissolved the *École freudienne de Paris*, his *agalma*, his own organization, the very space of his collective life? He was well aware that only such a 'self-destructive' act could clear the terrain for a new beginning.

The fact that all the above-quoted examples refer to male acts might lead to the conclusion that such a gesture is inherently masculine: in contrast to the masculine readiness to cut links, a woman remains rooted in her specific substance. . . . What, however, if the lesson of psychoanalysis is not only that such an act is gender-neutral, but even that the opposite is the case? So how can a woman subjectivize herself through such an act of 'shooting at herself'? The first association here, of course, is the standard feminist point: in order to become a *subject*, a woman has to eschew the very core of her 'femininity', that mysterious *je ne sais quoi*, something 'in her more than herself', the secret treasure [*agalma*] that makes her the *object* of male desire. However, there is another – perhaps more radical – point to be made here. That is to say: Lacan proposed as (one of) the definition(s) of 'a true woman' a certain radical *act*: the act of taking from man, her partner, of obliterating – even destroying – that which is 'in him more than himself', that which 'means everything to him' and which is more important to him than his own life, the precious *agalma* around which his life revolves. As the exemplary figure of such an act in literature, of course, Lacan cites Medea who, upon learning that Jason, her husband, plans to abandon her for a younger woman, kills their two young children, her husband's most precious possession – it is in this horrible act of destroying that which matters most to her husband that she acts as *une vraie femme*, as Lacan put it.[99]

So perhaps it is time, against the overblown celebration of Antigone, to reassert *Medea*, her uncanny, disturbing counterpart, as the subject of an authentic *act* – in a tradition that comes right down to Toni Morrison's *Beloved*, the novel about the unbearably painful birth of African-American subjectivity. As is well known, *Beloved* focuses on the traumatic desperate act of the heroine, Sethe: after she has escaped slavery with her four children, and enjoyed a month of calm recuperation with her mother-in-law in Cincinnati, the cruel overseer of the plantation from which she escaped attempts to capture her by appeal to the Fugitive Slave Law. Finding herself in this hopeless situation, without any prospect of escaping a return to slavery, Sethe resorts to a radical measure in order to spare her children a return to bondage: she cuts the throat of her eldest daughter, tries to kill her two sons, and threatens to dash out the brains of her infant daughter – in short, she commits a Medean *act* of trying to exterminate what is most precious to her, her progeny.[100] In an unsurpassed piece of cruel irony, this desperate assertion of freedom is interpreted by the white schoolteacher as proof that if African-Americans are given even a little too much freedom, they regress to African savagery – as if precisely such an act were not totally unthinkable within the mores of the African tribes from which the slaves were descended. . . .

Crucial to an understanding of Sethe's desperate measures are her later apparently paradoxical musings, where she declares: 'If I hadn't killed her she would have died, and that is something I could not bear to happen to her.'[101] Killing her daughter was the only way to preserve the minimal dignity of her life – or, as Morrison herself put it in an interview apropos of *Beloved* – by what may seem the ultimate cruelty of killing her offspring,

'Sethe is claiming her role as a parent, claiming the autonomy, the freedom she needs to protect her children and give them some dignity.'[102] In short, in a radical situation of forced choice in which, because of the relations of slavery, Sethe's children 'weren't *hers* at all',[103] the only way open to her to act effectively as a parent, protect her children and save their dignity, is to *kill* them.

This radical character of Sethe's act becomes apparent if we compare it with what is perhaps one of its literary models, Williams Styron's *Sophie's Choice*, in which the heroine, confronted with the choice of saving one of her two children from the gas chamber and renouncing the other, concedes to this blackmail by the Nazi officer and surrenders her older child, a daughter, in order to save her young son – with the predictable result that the guilt for this choice haunts her to the end of her life, driving her to suicide years later.

Although Sethe's traumatic act also continues to haunt her for decades (the 'Beloved' of the novel's title is none other than the ghost of the murdered daughter, who claws at the family's nerves like a relentless harpy, playing emotional and sexual games with all of them), what we are dealing with here is of precisely the opposite nature to *Sophie's Choice*: while Sophie's guilt results from her compromising attitude of accepting the terms of the Nazi officer's impossible choice, and choosing one child against the other, Sethe is haunted because she did *not* compromise her desire, but fully assumed the impossible–traumatic act of 'taking a shot at herself', at what was most precious to herself. Only at the end of the novel does the Beloved's withdrawal signal Sethe's ability to come to terms with the properly *ethical* monstrosity of her act.[104]

Sethe's act is an exemplary case of the properly *modern* ethical act which, according to Lacan, displays the structure of what Freud called the gesture of *abstaining* [*Versagung*].[105] In the traditional (premodern) act, the subject sacrifices everything (all 'pathological' things) for the Cause–Thing that matters to him more than life itself: Antigone, condemned to death, enumerates all the things she will *not* be able to experience because of her premature death (marriage, children . . .) – this is the 'bad infinity' one sacrifices through the Exception (the Thing for which one acts, and which, precisely, is *not* sacrificed). Here the structure is that of the Kantian Sublime: the overwhelming infinity of sacrificed empirical/pathological objects brings home in a negative way the enormous, incomprehensible dimension of the Thing for which one sacrifices them. So Antigone is sublime in her sad enumeration of what she is sacrificing – this list, in its enormity, indicates the transcendent contours of the Thing to which she retains her unconditional fidelity. Is it necessary to add that *this* Antigone is a *masculine* fantasy *par excellence*?

In the modern ethical constellation, on the contrary, one *suspends this exception of the Thing*: one bears witness to one's fidelity to the Thing by *sacrificing (also) the Thing itself* (in the same way, Kierkegaard enjoins a true Christian believer to hate the beloved himself out of love). And is this not the very unbearable crux of Sethe's act – that she killed her children *out of her very fidelity to them*, not as a 'primitive' act of brutal sacrificing to some obscure superego gods? Without this suspension, there is no ethical act proper.[106] So when we claim that the ethical act 'as such' has the structure of feminine subjectivity, and, furthermore, that the subject 'as such' is ultimately feminine, this does *not* involve the standard cliché about how men are involved in political power struggles, while women are inherently apolitical-ethical (as in the usual misreading of Antigone as the defender of ethical family values against masculine political manipulations): this very elevation of Woman into the protectress of pure Ethics exempted from masculine power struggles – who, as such, holds these struggles back, prevents them from exploding into the limitless search for power that violates every human consideration – is masculine in its inherent logic. In contrast to this ('masculine') universality of the struggle for power that relies on the ethical figure of Woman as its inherent exception, the ('feminine') ethical act proper involves precisely the *suspension* of this exception: it takes place in the *intersection* of ethics and politics, in the uncanny domain in which ethics is 'politicized' in its innermost nature, an affair of radically contingent decisions, a gesture that can no longer be accounted for in terms of fidelity to some pre-existing Cause, since it redefines the very terms of this Cause.

In short, the two opposed ways to read the relationship between ethics and politics precisely fit the Lacanian opposition between masculine and feminine 'formulae of sexuation': the very elevation of the Feminine stance into an apolitical ethical stance, safeguarding the male world of power politics from criminal excess, is inherently *masculine*; while the 'feminine' ethical act involves precisely the suspension of this boundary – that is to say, it has the structure of a *political* decision.[107] Yes, what makes Sethe's act so monstrous is the 'suspension of the ethical' involved in it, and this suspension *is* 'political' in the precise sense of an abyssal excessive gesture that can no longer be grounded in 'common human considerations'. In his reading of *Antigone*, Lacan emphasizes how, after her excommunication from the community, Antigone enters the domain of *ate*, of the unspeakable horror of dwelling 'between the two deaths', still alive yet excluded from the symbolic community – does not the same hold for Sethe? Morrison herself, in an interview, claimed that

> she has stepped across the line, so to speak. It's understandable, but it is excessive. This is what the townspeople in Cincinnati respond to, not her grief, but her arrogance. . . . They abandon her because of what they felt was her pride. Her statement about what is valuable to her – in a sense it damns what they think is valuable to them. They have had losses too. In her unwillingness to apologize or bend . . . she would kill her child again is what they know. That is what separates her from the rest of her community.[108]

In short, what makes Sethe so monstrous is not her act as such, but the way she refuses to 'relativize' it, to shed her responsibility for it, to concede that she acted in an unforgivable fit of despair or madness – instead of compromising her desire by assuming a distance towards her act, qualifying it as something 'pathological' (in the Kantian sense of the term), she insists on the radically ethical status of her monstrous deed.

Would not an adequate example of the same gesture from today's political life be the way the Serbs relate to Kosovo as their precious object–treasure, as the cradle of their civilization, as that which matters to them more than anything else, and which they are never able to renounce? Therein lies the final limit of the large majority of the so-called 'democratic opposition' to the Milošević regime: they unconditionally endorse Milošević's anti-Albanian nationalist agenda, even accusing him of making compromises with the West and 'betraying' Serb national interests in Kosovo. For this very reason, the *sine qua non* of an authentic act in Serbia today would be precisely to *renounce* the claim to Kosovo, to sacrifice the substantial attachment to the privileged object. (What we have here, therefore, is a nice case of the political dialectic of democracy: although democracy should be the ultimate goal of political activity in today's Serbia, any advocacy of democracy which does not explicitly renounce nationalistic claims to Kosovo is doomed to fail – *the* issue apropos of which the struggle for democracy will be decided is that of Kosovo.)

And – to go to the limit – is not the ultimate example of such a gesture of 'shooting at oneself', renouncing what is most precious to oneself, again provided by Christianity itself, by the Crucifixion? As Hegel emphasized, it is totally misleading to reduce the death of Christ to a sacrificial gesture in the exchange between God and man – to claim that by sacrificing that which is most precious to Himself, his own son, God redeems humanity, ransoming its sins. If we adopt this traditional stance, the question arises immediately: *for whom* – for which authority above Himself – is God Himself forced to sacrifice his son? Or is He playing perverse games with Himself – and, consequently, with us humans? So when the Bible proclaims that God sacrificed His only-begotten son to redeem humanity from its sins, there are only two ways to explain this strange act:[109]

- God as omnipotent is a *perverse* subject who plays obscene games with humanity and His own son: He creates suffering, sin and imperfection, so that He can intervene and resolve the mess He created, thereby securing for Himself the eternal gratitude of the human race;

- God is not omnipotent; He is like a Greek tragic hero sub-ordinated to a higher Destiny: His act of creation, like the fateful deed of the Greek hero, brings about unwanted dire conse-quences, and the only way for Him to re-establish the balance of Justice is to sacrifice what is most precious to Him, His own son – in this sense, God Himself is the ultimate Abraham.

The traditional reading thus obliterates the ultimate mystery of the Crucifixion: the Crucifixion, the death of the son of God, is a *happy* event – in it, the very structure of sacrifice, as it were, sub-lates itself, giving birth to a new subject no longer rooted in a particular substance, redeemed of all particular links (the 'Holy Spirit'). From this supreme example, it should also be clear that the necessity of renunciation inherent to the notion of act in no way entails that every utopian imagination gets caught in the trap of inherent transgression: when we abandon the fantasmatic Otherness which makes life in constrained social reality bearable, we catch a glimpse of Another Space which can no longer be dis-missed as a fantasmatic supplement to social reality.

The duet from *The Marriage of Figaro* in *The Shawshank Redemption* (the cinema version of King's story) is an exemplary case of the effect of the sublime which relies on the contrast between the poverty and horror of real life and the sudden intrusion of this Other Space. The black convict (Morgan Freeman), whose com-mentary we hear, claims that he doesn't know what the two ladies are singing about, and it is perhaps better that he doesn't know, but all the men listening to them were, for a brief moment, free. . . . What we have here is the effect of the sublime at its purest: the momentary suspension of meaning which elevates the subject into another dimension in which the prison terror has no hold over him. It is deeply significant that the duet is from Mozart (and, incidentally, a rather trifling one: the duet from Act III in which the Countess dictates to Susanna the letter destined to trap her unfaithful husband) – can one imagine a more startling contrast than the one between mid-twentieth-century American prison life and the universe of late-eighteenth-century aristocratic love intrigue? So the true contrast is not simply between the prison horror and the 'divine' Mozart's music but, within music itself, between the sublime dimension of music and the trifling character of its content. More precisely, what makes the scene sublime is that the poor prisoners, unaware of this trifling content, directly perceive the sublime beauty of the music. In other words, if we were to hear an overtly 'sublime' piece of music (like the fourth movement of Beethoven's Ninth), the effect would undoubtedly be pathetic in an extremely vulgar way.

The last words of the dying Tristan in Wagner's opera are 'What, *hear I the light*?'. This paradoxical short circuit between the two senses is what happens to the prisoners in this scene: in listening to Mozart's aria, they also *hear the light* – a proper revolutionary utopia always involves such a short circuit, in opposition to the reactionary obscene call of the superego in which, in the figure of the Leader, we *see the voice*. It should thus be clear how the standard notion of artistic beauty as a utopian false escape from the constraints of reality falls short: one should distinguish between ordinary escapism and this dimension of Otherness, this magic moment when *the Absolute appears* in all its fragility: the man who puts on the record in the prison (Tim Robbins) is precisely the one who rejects all false dreams about escaping from prison, about life Outside. . . .[110] In hearing this aria from *Figaro*, the prisoners have seen a ghost – neither the resuscitated obscene ghost of the past, not the spectral ghost of the capitalist present, but the brief apparition of a future utopian Otherness to which every authentic revolutionary stance should cling.

This, then, brings us back to our starting point: the third modality of ghosts is none other than the Holy Ghost itself, the community of believers *qua* 'uncoupled' outcasts from the social order – with, ideally, authentic psychoanalytic and revolutionary political collectives as its two main forms. And if there is often something monstrous about encountering such ghosts (since, as we know from Rilke, beauty is the last veil that envelops the Monstrous) – if, after such encounters, we actually *look as if we have seen a ghost* – we should remember Heiner Müller's famous motto: 'The first appearance of the new is the dread'.

NOTES

1. See Alain Badiou, *Saint Paul ou la naissance de l'universalisme*, Paris: PUF 1998.

2. See Vesna Goldworth, *Inventing Ruritania*, New Haven, CT and London: Yale University Press 1998.

3. Ibid.

4. See Étienne Balibar, 'La Violence: idéalité et cruauté', in *La crainte des masses*, Paris: Éditions Galilée 1997.

5. For a more detailed development of this theme, see Chapter 3 of Slavoj Žižek, *The Metastases of Enjoyment*, London and New York: Verso 1995; and Chapter 6 of *The Ticklish Subject*, London and New York: Verso 1999.

6. Karl Marx and Frederick Engels, *The Communist Manifesto*, Harmondsworth: Penguin 1985, pp. 83–4.

7. Ibid., p. 82.

8. See Henry Krips, *Fetish: An Erotics of Culture*, Ithaca, NY: Cornell University Press 1999.

9. And does not the same often go for the parents themselves? Recall the proverbial suitor who, in order to impress his future father-in-law, engages in such intense conversation with him that at a certain point his poor fiancée explodes: 'Where am I in all this? I feel like a disturbing element – why don't the two of you just go away and forget about me?'

10. In the last years of Communism in Eastern Europe, for example, democracy was desirable, but *through* the intermediary of Communist constraints – once this intermediate obstacle fell, we got the object of our desire, but deprived of its cause.

11. And is not something similar taking place, on a wholly different level, with the IMF's help to developing Third World nations? Is it not true that the more such a state accepts IMF help, and obeys its conditions or takes its advice, the more it becomes dependent on the IMF, and the more help it needs?

12. The notorious Iraqi 'weapons of mass destruction' offer another example of the *objet petit a*: they are an elusive entity, never empirically specified, a kind of Hitchcockian MacGuffin, expected to be hidden in the most disparate and improbable places, from the (rather logical) desert to the (slightly irrational) cellars of presidential palaces (so that when the palace is bombed, they may poison Saddam and his entire entourage); allegedly present in large quantities, yet magically moved around all the time by workers; and the more they are destroyed, the more all-present and all-powerful they are in their threat, as if the removal of the greater part of them magically heightens the destructive power of the remainder – as such, by definition they can never be found, and are therefore all the more dangerous. . . .

13. This tendency often leads to the comic confusion whereby a work of art is mistaken for an everyday object, or vice versa. Recently, in Potsdamerplatz, the largest construction site in Berlin, the co-ordinated movement of dozens of gigantic cranes was staged as an art performance – doubtless perceived by many uninformed passers-by as part of an intense construction activity. . . . I myself made the opposite blunder during a trip to Berlin: I noticed along and above all the main streets numerous large blue tubes and pipes, as if the intricate cobweb of water, phone, electricity, and so on, was no longer hidden beneath the earth, but displayed in public. My reaction was, of course, that this was probably another of those postmodern art performances whose aim was, this time, to reveal the intestines of the town, its hidden inner machinery, in a kind of equivalent to displaying on video the palpitation of our stomach or lungs – I was soon proved wrong, however, when friends pointed out to me that what I saw was merely part of the standard maintenance and repair of the city's underground service network.

14. It is worth noting that it is Lacanian theory, with its link between surplus-enjoyment and surplus-value, which offers the best theoretical frame for grasping this new trend, with respect to the fact that one of the

standard criticisms of Lacan is that his theory is abstract, proto-Kantian, dealing with the ahistorical symbolic system, unaware of the concrete socio-historical conditions of its subject matter. We can see apropos of our example how, in clear contrast to this criticism, the cultural studies which celebrate new multiple perverse forms of artistic production do not take sufficiently into account how these phenomena are grounded in global capitalism, with its accelerated commodification – it is Lacanian theory that enables us fully to conceptualize this link, effectively to rehistoricize the topics of cultural studies.

15. Gilles Deleuze, *The Logic of Sense*, New York: Columbia University Press 1987, p. 41; see also Chapter 5 of Žižek, *The Metastases of Enjoyment*.

16. Perhaps one way to imagine this notion of 'nothing but the place taking place' is the experience of seeing that the paper spewed out by the fax machine is blank: does this blankness mean that the machine has simply *malfunctioned*, that the text typed on the paper at the other end was not transmitted, *or* that the person at the other end (by mistake, in all probability) put *a blank piece of paper* into the machine (or inserted the paper with the wrong – blank – side down)? Do we not encounter here a kind of mechanical counterpart to the Nietzschean distinction between 'willing nothing' and '[actively] willing the nothingness itself': the blank paper can mean 'the message didn't get through' or 'the void we see *is* the message the sender put in'? So how do we decide? By looking closely at the paper: if there are tiny stains on it, meaningless material leftovers, it means that the void *is* the message, that is, that 'nothing but the place took place' – it was not that 'nothing took place', since, in a way, the empty place itself took place. . . .

17. See Gérard Wajcman, *L'objet du siècle*, Lagrasse: Verdier 1998.

18. Quoted from Julia Hell, *Post-Fascist Fantasies*, Durham, NC: Duke University Press 1997, p. 32.

19. Kim Yong Il is hailed by the official propaganda as 'witty' and 'poetic' – an example of his poetry: 'In the same way as sunflowers can blossom and thrive only if they are turned up and look towards the sun, people can thrive only if they look up towards their leader!'

20. Jacques Lacan, *The Ethics of Psychoanalysis*, London: Routledge 1992, p. 149.

21. Ibid., p. 150. Translation corrected.

22. It is against this background that one should appreciate the early (Soviet) paintings of Komar and Melamid, as exemplified in their 'Stalin and the Muses': they combine in one and the same painting two incompatible notions of beauty: 'real' beauty – the classicist notion of Ancient Greek beauty as the lost ideal of organic innocence (the Muses) – and the purely 'functional' beauty of the Communist leader. Their ironically subversive effect does not lie only in the grotesque contrast and incongruity of the two levels, but – perhaps even more – in the suspicion that Ancient Greek beauty itself was not as 'natural' as it may appear to us, but conditioned by a certain functional framework.

23. In this reference to Courbet, I draw extensively on Charity Scribner, 'Working Memory: Mourning and Melancholia in Postindustrial Europe', dissertation, Columbia University, 2000.

24. Francis Scott Fitzgerald, *The Last Tycoon*, Harmondsworth: Penguin 1960, p. 51.

25. Another way to approach the dead end of premodernist art is perhaps embodied in the pre-Raphaelite movement: the sublime beauty in their paintings which is dangerously close to kitsch, is, as it were, undermined from within by the excessive accent on detail – the first effect of sublime and ethereal beauty starts to disintegrate as one gradually becomes aware of the intense details that seem to lead a life of their own, and thus somehow introduce a note of voluptuous overripe vulgarity into the whole of the painting.

26. This passage from the direct expression of the incestuous object-turned-abject to abstraction is most evidently at work in the artistic development of Mark Rothko, whose famous intensely coloured abstract paintings were preceded by a series of direct portraits of his mother. One is tempted to conceive of Rothko's late abstract paintings as a kind of transposition-into-colour of Malevich's 'Black Square': the basic spatial co-ordinates are the same (central square against background); the key difference is simply that in Rothko's work colour does not simply shade the contours of the drawn objects but, rather, functions directly as the medium of drawing, of presenting these contours – Rothko does not colour drawn shapes, he draws shapes directly (or rather, *sees* shapes) with colours.

27. Jacques-Alain Miller, 'The Desire of Lacan', *Lacanian ink* 14, Spring 1999, p. 19.

28. Heiner Müller and Jan Hoet, 'Insights into the Process of Production: A Conversation', *documenta IX*, vol. I, Stuttgart: Edition Cantz 1992, pp. 96–7.

29. Scribner, 'Working Memory', p. 150.

30. See Jacques Lacan, *Le Séminaire, livre VIII: Le transfert*, Paris: Éditions du Seuil 1991.

31. G.W.F. Hegel, *Phenomenology of Spirit*, Oxford: Oxford University Press 1977, pp. 317–18.

32. Jacques Derrida, *Of Grammatology*, Baltimore, MD: Johns Hopkins University Press 1976, pp. 68–9.

33. Hegel, *Phenomenology of Spirit*, p. 404.

34. See Carl Jensen, *Censored 1999: The News That Didn't Make the News*, New York: Seven Stories Press 1999.

35. Václav Havel, 'Kosovo and the End of the Nation-State', *New York Review of Books*, vol. XLVI, no. 10 (10 June 1999), p. 6.

36. Ibid.

37. Steven Erlanger, 'In One Kosovo Woman, an Emblem of Suffering', *The New York Times*, 12 May 1999, p. A 13.

38. In this respect, Lafontaine's fall is a phenomenon parallel to the demise of the leaders of the Prague Spring of 1968: the Soviet intervention, in a way, saved their face – saved the illusion that, if allowed to stay in power they would actually have created 'socialism with a human face', an authentic alternative to both Real Socialism and Real Capitalism.

39. See Eric Santner, 'Traumatic Revelations: Freud's Moses and the Origins of Anti-Semitism', in Renata Salecl, ed., *Sexuation*, Durham, NC: Duke University Press 2000.

40. See René Girard, *The Scapegoat*, Baltimore, MD: Johns Hopkins University Press 1989.

41. See Sigmund Freud, *Moses and Monotheism*, Pelican Freud Library vol. 13, *The Origins of Religion*, Harmondsworth: Penguin 1983.

42. Santner, 'Traumatic Revelations', p. 78.

43. Jacques Lacan, *Seminar XX: Encore*, New York: Norton 1998, p. 59.

44. I owe this story to George Rosenwald, University of Michigan, Ann Arbor.

45. See Ian Hacking, *Rewriting the Soul*, Princeton, NJ: Princeton University Press 1995.

46. *Film Noir*, ed. Alain Silver and Elizabeth Ward, London: Secker & Warburg 1980, p. 297.

47. Ibid., p. 298.

48. I take this term from Judith Butler – see *The Psychic Life of Power*, Stanford, CA: Stanford University Press 1998.

49. See F.W.J. von Schelling, *Ages of the World*/Slavoj Žižek, *The Abyss of Freedom*, Ann Arbor: University of Michigan Press 1997.

50. Ibid., pp. 181–2.

51. See Binjamin Wilkomirski, *Fragments: Memories of a Wartime Childhood*, New York: Schocken 1996.

52. See John Sallis, 'Deformatives: Essentially Other Than Truth', in John Sallis, ed., *Reading Heidegger*, Bloomington: Indiana University Press 1993.

53. Friedrich Nietzsche, *Der Wille zur Macht*, Stuttgart: Alfred Kröner 1959, para. 493.

54. See Jacques Lacan, *Écrits*, Paris: Éditions du Seuil 1966, p. 807.

55. William Richardson, 'Heidegger among the Doctors', in Sallis, ed., *Reading Heidegger*, p. 62. Here, incidentally, Richardson clearly contradicts his own claim two pages earlier that 'Lacan's question about the structure of the unconscious in psychoanalysis is clearly an existential/ontic one (i.e. on the level of beings)' (p. 60) and, as such, unable to render thematic the fundamental–ontological question of the Sense of Being: how can a term which concerns the very kernel of the essence of truth (the Lacanian 'Real') not bear upon this ontological question?

56. Martin Heidegger, *Beiträge zur Philosophie*, in *Gesamtausgabe*, Frankfurt: Vittorio Klostermann 1975– , vol. 65, p. 338.

57. In a broader context, one should approach here the general theme of 'East versus West' – of the global difference between 'Eastern' and 'Western' elementary symbolic matrixes. In the 'Eastern' perspective at its most radical, the ultimate 'reality' is that of Emptiness, of the 'positive Void', and all finite/determinate reality is inherently 'illusory' – the only authentic way to ethico-epistemological Truth is to renounce desire as the condition which chains us to finite objects, and is thus the ultimate cause of suffering – that is, to enter the impassive bliss of nirvana. In contrast to this stance, the innermost core of the 'Western' matrix is that *there is a third way*: to put it in

Kantian-Nietzschean terms, the alternative between 'not desiring anything' and the 'pathological' desire that chains us to positive empirical objects is not exhaustive, since there is in humans a desire which is not 'pathological', but a 'pure' desire for nothingness itself. Or – to put it in Heidegger's terms (since in his notion of primordial *lethe*, Heidegger is ultimately getting at the same point) – a 'pre-ontological derangement' is consubstantial with the human condition itself, more 'original' than the alternative between blissful immersion in the Void and enslavement to 'pathological' desires.

The Lacanian position on the Oriental notion of nirvana is therefore clear and unequivocal: the ultimate choice we, desiring humans, are facing is not the choice between desire (for something within false reality) and renunciation (extinction) of desire, not desiring, immersion in the Void; there is a third option: the desire for Nothingness itself, for an object which is a stand-in for this Nothingness. The Lacanian position is not that Buddhism is 'too strong', that it is only for those who are able effectively to extinguish their desire; while for us Western subjects, caught in the dialectic of desire, psychoanalysis is as far as we can go – it is that the 'desire for Nothingness itself' is the 'vanishing mediator', the third, more primordial option, which becomes invisible once we formulate the opposition as that between desire for something and not desiring. The existence of this third option is discernible in the difficulty a Buddhist position has in explaining the emergence of desire: how is it that the primordial Void was disturbed, and that desire emerged; that living beings got caught up in the wheel of karma, of attachment to false reality? The only solution to this deadlock is to posit a kind of pre-ontological perturbation/inversion/disturbance *within nirvana itself* – that is to say, prior to the split between nirvana and false appearance – so that the Absolute itself (the cosmic Force, or whatever it is called) gets radically perverted. The traces of this inversion are discernible even in pop-cultural New Age icons like Darth Vader from *Star Wars*: in the idea that the truly evil people are those who have gained access to the Force that enables us to reach the true realm beyond false material reality, but then perverted/misused this Force, employing it for bad, evil ends. What, however, if this fall into perversion is original, the original monstrous cut/excess, and the opposition between nirvana and desire for false appearances is there to conceal this monstrosity?

58. I have dealt with this problem in detail in *The Indivisible Remainder* (London and New York: Verso 1996) and in *The Ticklish Subject*. The point to emphasize here is that Heidegger's attempt to 'pass through' modern-age subjectivity has nothing whatsoever to do with the New Age cliché, according to which the original sin of modern Western civilization (or, indeed, of the Judaeo-Christian tradition) is man's *hubris*, his arrogant assumption that he occupies the central place in the universe and/or that he is endowed with the Divine right to master all other beings and exploit them for his own benefit. The idea is that this *hubris* which disturbs the delicate balance of cosmic powers forces Nature sooner or later to re-establish this balance: today's ecological, social and psychic crisis is interpreted as the universe's justified answer to man's presumption. Our only solution thus consists of a shift in the global paradigm, in adopting the new holistic attitude in which we humbly accept our subordinate place in the global Order of Being. . . . In clear contrast to this notion that underlies all returns to 'ancient wisdom', Heidegger is fully aware that the '*derangement* of man's position among beings', the fact that man's emergence somehow 'derails' the balance of entities, is in a way *older than Truth itself*, its very hidden foundation. One should therefore reject entirely Reiner Schürmann's reading according to which the Heideggerian 'forgetting of Being' – the metaphysical oblivion of ontological difference, that is, confusion between the event–horizon of Being as such and the Supreme Entity – equals the disturbing of cosmic balance, the privileging of one aspect of the cosmic antagonism in favour of its opposite, thus elevating it into a universal Principle (see Reiner Schürmann, 'Ultimate Double Binds', *Graduate Faculty Philosophy Journal*, New York: New School for Social Research, vol. 14, no. 2): for Heidegger, the Truth-Event can occur only within such a fundamental 'ontological imbalance'. The truly problematic and central point is that Heidegger refuses to call this 'ontological imbalance' or 'derangement' *subject*.

59. For a more detailed elaboration of the concept of the death drive, see Chapter 5 of Žižek, *The Ticklish Subject*.

60. Daniel C. Dennett, *Consciousness Explained*, New York: Little, Brown 1991, p. 132. (Dennett, of course, evokes this concept in a purely negative way, as a nonsensical *contradictio in adjecto*.)

61. For a more detailed account of this notion of fundamental fantasy, see Chapters 1 and 4 of Slavoj Žižek, *The Plague of Fantasies*, London and New York: Verso 1997.

62. Martin Heidegger, *The Fundamental Concepts of Metaphysics*, Bloomington: Indiana University Press 1995, p. 271.

63. On this notion of the act, see Chapter 1 of Žižek, *The Indivisible Remainder*.

64. See Ernesto Laclau, *Emancipation(s)*, London and New York: Verso 1995.

65. One is tempted to interpret Heidegger's passage from his early proto-transcendental 'analytic of *Dasein*' to his later concept of the History of Being along the same lines: is not the non-historical kernel of this historicity Heidegger's unresolved trauma of his Nazi political engagement? As for Heidegger's *silence* after the war, his persistent refusal to settle his accounts with his past in public, unambiguously to condemn Nazism and his role in it – is this silence not *telling*, bearing unequivocal witness to his remaining traumatic 'passionate attachment' to the Nazi dream, to the fact that he never really got over it, acquired a distance towards it, 'put his Nazi past at rest'? No, Heidegger did not simply 'repress' or 'erase' his past political engagement: his withdrawal from public life in his later years proves, rather, that the wound was still raging, that the subject was still hot and extremely touchy, that is to say, the only imaginable political engagement for him was the Nazi engagement, the only alternative being withdrawal into pure thought (rather like a deceived lover who, disappointed when he is betrayed by his mistress, abstains from any further sexual contact, that is, cannot move on to *other* women, and thus, in his very *universal* hatred of sexual relations, bears witness to the fact that he is still traumatically scarred by the *one* failed contact).

66. See Book One of Immanuel Kant, *Religion Within the Limits of Reason Alone*, New York: Harper & Row 1960.

67. See Michel Foucault, *The History of Sexuality, Volume I: An Introduction*, Harmondsworth: Penguin 1981. Again, I owe this point to Eric Santner (private conversation).

68. In the history of Christianity we have, in the unique spiritual moment of the twelfth century, two interconnected subversions of this opposition

between *eros* and *agape*: the Cathar version of Christianity and the emergence of courtly love. It is no wonder that, although opposed, they are part of the same historical movement – they both involve a kind of short circuit which, from the strict Pauline standpoint, has to appear as illegitimate. The basic operation of courtly love was to *retranslate agape back into eros*: to redefine sexual love itself as the ultimate, unending ethical Duty, to elevate *eros* to the level of the sublime *agape*. The Cathars, in contrast, thoroughly rejected *eros* as such – for them, the opposition between *eros* and *agape* was elevated into a Gnostic–dualistic cosmic polarity: no 'moderate' permissible sexuality is possible; every sexual act, even with a legitimate spouse, is ultimately incestuous, since it serves the propagation and reproduction of terrestrial life, and *this* world is the work of Satan – for the Cathars, the God who, at the very beginning of the Bible, says 'Let there be light!' is none other than Satan himself.

69. G.W.F. Hegel, 'Jenaer Realphilosophie', in *Frühe politische Systeme*, Frankfurt: Ullstein 1974, p. 204; translation quoted from Donald Phillip Verene, *Hegel's Recollection*, Albany, NY: SUNY Press 1985, pp. 7–8. For a closer reading of this passage see Chapter 1 of Žižek, *The Ticklish Subject*.

70. In this reading of Kieslowski's *Blue*, I draw again on Scribner, 'Working Memory'.

71. See Butler's systematic critical reading of Lacan in *Bodies That Matter*, New York: Routledge 1993, pp. 57–91.

72. Ernesto Laclau, *The Politics of Rhetoric*, intervention at the conference 'Culture and Materiality', University of California, Davis, 23–25 April 1998.

73. Lacan's concept of sublimation is the result of a very simple yet radical operation: he brings together the Freudian problematic of 'sublimation' (which, to put it in somewhat simplified terms, involves shifting the libido from an object that satisfies some immediate material need to an object that has no apparent connection to this need: destructive literary criticism becomes sublimated aggressivity; scientific research on the human body becomes sublimated voyeurism . . .) and the Kantian notion of the 'Sublime' (an empirical object/event which, through its very failure adequately to represent the noumenal Idea, evokes this trans-phenomenal Idea, as in the famous notion of extreme natural phenomena like storms and earthquakes which, in their very majesty, fail to represent the noumenal free-

dom adequately, and thus give birth to the reasoning: 'even Nature at its mightiest is infinitely less than my freedom').

Lacan replaces the Kantian noumenal Thing with the impossible/real Thing, the ultimate object of desire – the primordial movement of 'sublimation' is thus not from concrete material sexual, etc., needs to 'spiritual' concerns, but the shifting of the libido from the void of the 'unserviceable' Thing to some concrete, material object of need which assumes a sublime quality the moment it occupies the place of the Thing. This is why Lacan defines sublimation as the elevation of an object into the dignity of the Thing: 'sublimation' occurs when an object, part of everyday reality, finds itself in the place of the impossible Thing. This Thing is inherently anamorphic: it can be perceived only when it is viewed from the side, in a partial, distorted form, as its own shadow – if we look straight at it we see nothing, a mere void. (In a homologous way, we could speak of temporal anamorphosis: the Thing is attainable only by an incessant postponement, as its absent point-of-reference.) The Thing is therefore literally something that is created – whose place is encircled – through a network of detours, approximations and near-misses.

74. See Theodor W. Adorno, *Drei Studien zu Hegel*, Frankfurt: Suhrkamp 1963, p. 13.

75. Here I draw on Julia Reinhard Lupton (UC Irvine) and Kenneth Reinhard (UCLA)'s unpublished paper 'The Subject of Religion: Lacan and the Ten Commandments'.

76. In this context, Lacan himself draws attention to the resistance to the use of lie-detectors in crime investigations – as if such a direct 'objective' verification somehow infringes on the subject's right to the privacy of his thoughts.

77. See Paul Moyaert, 'Lacan on Neighborly Love', *Epoche* no. 1, 1996, Providence (UT), pp. 1–31.

78. On this notion, see Chapter 3 of Žižek, *The Metastases of Enjoyment*.

79. Lacan, *The Ethics of Psychoanalysis*, p. 81.

80. See Donald Davidson, *Inquiries into Truth and Interpretation*, Oxford: Clarendon Press 1984, p. 137.

81. Ibid.

82. Ibid., pp. 168–9.

83. Ibid., p. 197.

84. See Lacan, *Seminar XX: Encore.*

85. I owe this point to a conversation with Alenka Zupančič. To give another example: that was also the deadlock of the 'open marriage' relationship between Jean-Paul Sartre and Simone de Beauvoir: it is clear from reading their letters that their 'pact' was in fact asymmetrical and did not work, causing de Beauvoir many traumas. She expected that although Sartre had a series of other lovers, she was none the less the Exception, the one true love connection; while for Sartre, it was not that she was just one in the series, but that she was precisely *one of the exceptions* – that his series was a series of women each of whom was 'something exceptional' to him. . . .

86. Does not this passage from the external tension between the Law and the series of 'pathological' symptoms as the indices of the failure of the Law to the space in which there are *only* symptoms repeat the basic matrix of the Hegelian criticism of Kant, in which the condition of impossibility (the 'pathological' obstacle that forever prevents the realization of the Law) coincides with the condition of *possibility*: what the Law perceives as the obstacle to its full actualization is the very condition of its functioning, so that, the Law, by fighting the symptoms too strongly, undermines its own foundation? In other words, the gap between the Law and its symptoms is now posited as internal to the symptoms themselves (just as, in Hegel's logic, the Universal itself is one of its own particular species).

87. Søren Kierkegaard, *Works of Love*, New York: Harper Torchbooks 1962, p. 114.

88. Ibid., p. 221.

89. I have dealt with this opposition in practically all my latest books; see, for example, Chapter 3 of Žižek, *The Metastases of Enjoyment.*

90. Lacan, *The Ethics of Psychoanalysis*, p. 73.

91. The Frankfurt School tradition discerned this key feature of the libidinal structure of 'totalitarianism' in the guise of the hypothesis of *repressive desublimation*; on the difference between the Frankfurt School approach and the Lacanian approach with regard to this feature, see Chapter 1 of Žižek, *The Metastases of Enjoyment.*

92. Aleksandar Tijanić, 'The Remote Day of Change', *Mladina* (Ljubljana), 9 August 1999, p. 33.

93. The next step here would be to oppose the 'totalitarian' to the liberal-permissive *You may!*. In both cases, the message is: 'You may . . . possess the object *without paying the proper price for desire, for desiring it.*' And in both cases, this avoidance of paying the price for desire exacts a price of its own. In permissive liberalism, the 'You may!' of freely inventing your Self becomes entangled in the intricate web of prohibitions concerning the well-being of yourself and your neighbours (what not to eat and drink, the rules of safe sex, the prohibition against injuring the Other . . .); in a precisely symmetrical way, the totalitarian 'You may . . .' (ignore your own and your neighbour's well-being) demands subordination to the figure of the Master.

94. Daniel C. Dennett, *Darwin's Dangerous Idea*, New York: Simon & Schuster 1996, p. 421.

95. See Oswald Ducrot, *Le dire et le dit*, Paris: Éditions du Seuil 1977.

96. We can see how the triad ISR (Imaginary–Symbolic–Real) is operative in these three readings of the transfusion example: the judge's procedure is Imaginary (providing a lie legitimized by the other's well-being); the second procedure, demanding subjective truth, relies on the Symbolic; while the third procedure generates a kind of knowledge in the Real.

97. For a closer reading of *Breaking the Waves*, see Slavoj Žižek, 'Death and the Maiden', in *The Žižek Reader*, Oxford: Blackwell 1998.

98. Kierkegaard, *Works of Love*, p. 102.

99. In his version of *Medea* (see 'Waterfront Wasteland Medea Material Landscape with Argonauts', in *Theatremachine*, London: Faber & Faber 1995), Heiner Müller recognized in Medea the ultimate figure of excessive revolutionary revenge against oppressive rulers. Furthermore, in his unique attempt to think *together* the necessity of revolutionary violence and the basic humanity that demands that we recognize the dignity of the dead, he proposed the unique phantasmic combination/condensation of Medea and Antigone: Medea, who first kills and dismembers her brother (in order to enable herself and Jason to escape their pursuers) and then – as Antigone does with her own brother – gently holds him in her arms. Here we have the image of the agent/executioner who, after accomplishing his terrible deed on behalf of the Revolution, takes upon himself the burden of guilt, and gently buries the dead. (Another such paradoxical Müllerian figure is that of

'Christ the Tiger' – of the Christ who first slaughters his enemy, then gently takes care of him.) The point to be noted here is that if the figure of Medea is to be reappropriated for the radical tradition, one should retain and reinscribe the very act which makes her so unpalatable to decent humanist consciousness: her ruthless killing of her own children (in contrast to Christa Wolf's otherwise outstanding *Medea*, in which she redeems Medea by reinterpreting her killing of her brother and children as a malicious rumour spread by her high-ranking enemies in order to discredit her).

100. As is well known, the comparison between Sethe and Medea was introduced by Stanley Crouch as a problematic feature in his 'Aunt Medea', a negative review of *Beloved*; Morrison herself rejected the comparison, claiming that Sethe 'didn't do what Medea did and kill her children because of some guy' (quoted from *Toni Morrison: Beloved*, [Icon Critical Guides], ed. Carl Plasa, Cambridge, MA: Icon Books 1998, p. 36). One is none the less tempted to claim that Morrison's dismissal of the comparison relies on a superficial reading of Medea's gesture.

101. Toni Morrison, *Beloved*, New York: Knopf 1987, p. 217.

102. Quoted from *Toni Morrison: Beloved*, p. 43.

103. Ibid.

104. On the level of narrative technique, this monstrosity of the act is signalled by the fact that the text approaches it only gradually: Sethe, with her murdered daughter, is first described from the perspective of the slave-catchers (who see in the murder the ultimate proof of her barbarity); then through the perspectives of other African-American witnesses (Baby Suggs, Stamp Paid); and even when the story of infanticide is finally told by Sethe herself, she finds it difficult to convey – well aware that she will be misunderstood – that her act is not something that can be integrated into 'common knowledge', that it is too monstrous to be narrated as a heroic mythical event. And, as Sally Keenan has suggested (see *Toni Morrison: Beloved*, p. 129), the same delayed encounter with the trauma is at work in the fact that it has only recently become possible to tell such a story: it was the modern emotional and political resonance of the theme of abortion that finally provided the proper background for it – with the additional twist, of course, that the infanticide in *Beloved* precisely subverts the standard opposition between the rights of the mother and those of the fetus, the opposition

which provides the co-ordinates for abortion debates: in *Beloved*, the infanticide is paradoxically justified by the rights of the child herself.

105. Here I draw on a conversation with Alenka Zupančič.

106. For a more detailed analysis of this structure of *Versagung*, see Chapter 2 of Žižek, *The Indivisible Remainder*.

107. And, incidentally, this structure of *Versagung* also provides an answer to the naïve, but necessary, question 'What does one actually *learn* in Brecht's learning plays?' – one learns the art of *Versagung*. This is why those interpreters of Brecht who claim that it is wrong to focus on the final act of forcedly chosen self-sacrifice of the young actor/person in *Der Jasager* or *Die Massnahme* miss the point. They emphasize that such a focus neglects the proper learning function of these plays, and reinscribes them in the standard *tragic* dramaturgy. *Versagung*, however, is the gesture of such a radical self-obliteration that it goes *beyond* the standard notion of what is 'tragic'.

108. Quoted from *Toni Morrison: Beloved*, p. 34.

109. If, of course, we take this statement at its face value – if we discard the standard Gnostic reading according to which the God who created our world was a half-impotent, slightly sadistic imbecile who made a botched job of creation, bringing about an imperfect world full of suffering; consequently, Christ expired in order to pay not for the sins of humanity but for the sins of his Father, of the Creator Himself.

110. The key dimension of Stephen King's story on which the film is based is indicated by its *title*: 'Rita Hayworth and the Shawshank Redemption'. Does not the apparently ridiculous plot (for long years the hero digs a hole in the wall – his escape tunnel – beneath a large poster of Rita Hayworth and other later film stars) provide the minimal matrix of the sublime: an image of beauty (the pin-up poster) which serves as the screen concealing the *hole*, the gap, which opens up a passage to freedom, out of the prison universe?

INDEX